# CONSUMER PROTECTION

*A Symposium*

# SYMPOSIA ON LAW AND SOCIETY

GENERAL EDITOR: LEONARD W. LEVY

*Claremont Graduate School*

# CONSUMER PROTECTION

## *A Symposium*

ALBERT L. CLOVIS     EDWARD J. MURPHY
HENRY J. BAILEY, III     MORRIS J. SHANKER
JOHN A. SPANOGLE, JR.     MARK A. ABEL
MERLIN G. MILLER

DA CAPO PRESS • NEW YORK • 1972

Library of Congress Cataloging in Publication Data

Main entry under title:
Consumer protection.

(Symposia on law and society)
"Appeared originally in the Ohio State law journal,
volume 29, number 3 (Summer 1968)"
    1. Consumer protection—Law and legislation—United
States—Addresses, essays, lectures. I. Clovis, Albert
L. II. Series.
KF1609.A2C65            343'.73'07            72-6757
ISBN 0-306-70524-9

The papers contained in this volume appeared originally in the *Ohio State Law Journal,* Volume 29, Number 3 (Summer 1968). They are reprinted by permission of the Editors of the *Ohio State Law Journal* and of the several authors. The Appendix to Professor Spanogle's essay has been prepared especially for this edition. For purposes of accurate citation, the original pagination of the symposium has been retained in square brackets.

Published by Da Capo Press, Inc.
A Subsidiary of Plenum Publishing Corporation
227 West 17th Street, New York, New York 10011

# CONTENTS

# CONSUMER PROTECTION SYMPOSIUM
## FOREWORD

ALBERT L. CLOVIS*

The consumer is no longer a forgotten man. At least not in the rhetoric of the day. In his 1968 State of the Union message, President Johnson called upon Congress to "make this truly a new day for the American consumer, and by giving him this protection we can live in history as the consumer conscious Congress."[1] Similar calls have issued and are issuing from state and local leaders across the nation. And there has been an outpouring of scholarly writing concerning the problems of the consumer, particularly the impoverished consumer.[2] Politically and intellectually, "consumer protection" has become one of the fashionable issues of the time.

Nor has this awakening interest in consumer problems been limited to talk; there has been action as well. The last few years have seen the enactment of a number of consumer-oriented federal statutes, the most recent and certainly not the least important of which is the Truth-in-Lending Act.[3] State legislatures have begun to move in a parallel direction. In 1966 and 1967, Massachusetts enacted two far-reaching pieces of consumer legislation.[4] And more seems to be in the offing, particularly the soon-to-be-promulgated Uniform Consumer Credit Code, which is the subject of the first two articles in this symposium. The rights of the poor consumer under existing law are also receiving increasing attention as legal assistance programs are enlarged and invigorated with federal funds.[5]

---

* Associate Professor of Law, The Ohio State University College of Law.

1 President Lyndon B. Johnson, State of the Union Message, Jan. 17, 1968, UNITED STATES CODE CONGRESSIONAL AND ADMINISTRATIVE NEWS, 90TH CONG., 2D SESS. 133, 137 (1968).

2 See, e.g., D. CAPLOVITZ, THE POOR PAY MORE (1963); NEW YORK UNIVERSITY SCHOOL OF LAW PROJECT ON SOCIAL WELFARE LAW, THE LAW AND THE LOW INCOME CONSUMER (1968); Symposium on Consumer Protection, 64 MICH. L. REV. 1197 (1966); Consumer Credit: A Symposium, 8 B.C. IND. AND COM. L. REV. 387 (1967).

3 82 Stat. 146, Pub. L. No. 90-321 (May 29, 1968).

4 Retail Installment Sales and Services Act, MASS. ANN. LAWS ch. 255D, §§ 1-31 (1968); Regulation of Business Practices for Consumer's Protection Act, MASS. ANN. LAWS ch. 93A, §§ 1-8 (Supp. 1967).

5 The activities of the Ohio State Legal Services Association, especially its recent publication of COURSE ON LAW AND POVERTY: THE CONSUMER, are illustrative of this development.

Judges, too, are becoming more consumer conscious, as a number of recent decisions attest.[6]

We are thus caught up in a consumer-rights movement. Whatever one's view of the significance of this movement's accomplishments to date, it must be conceded that those accomplishments are sufficient to command the attention of every lawyer of general interests. Moreover, the movement is clearly going, and clearly should go, further. The difficult and important questions are precisely how far and in what directions it should go. What must we do to achieve justice for the consumer? What actions will be ineffective or, worse, redound to the ultimate disadvantage of consumers by imposing unnecessary or exhorbitant costs on sellers and financers? In its own way, each of the articles in this symposium contributes to the answering of these questions.

Professor Bailey opens the symposium with a description of the most comprehensive piece of consumer legislation presently under serious consideration: the proposed Uniform Consumer Credit Code. Still in draft form, this product of the National Conference of Commissioners on Uniform State Laws is designed to replace, simplify and modernize a plethora of existing statutes, including retail installment sales acts, small loan acts and usury laws. In addition, it would work a number of reforms which would be of particular importance in Ohio. For example, it would make the familiar cognovit provision void when contained in a consumer note,[7] and it would go a long way toward depriving the financers of consumer sales of the ability to obtain holder-in-due-course status.

In connection with the last matter, it is interesting to note that Professor Bailey's view of the U3C's provision on negotiable notes differs from that subsequently taken by Professor Murphy. The section in question, 2.403, provides that:

> In a consumer credit sale or consumer lease . . . the seller or lessor may not take a negotiable promissory note payable in installments as evidence of the obligation of the buyer or lessee. A promissory note negotiable in form issued in violation of this section may be enforced as a negotiable instrument by a holder in due course according to its terms. . . .

Professor Bailey is concerned that in the event a seller takes a negotiable note in violation of the first sentence of this provision and

---

[6] *See, e.g.,* Williams v. Walker-Thomas Furniture Co., 350 F.2d 445 (D.C. Cir. 1965); Unico v. Owen, 50 N.J. 101, 232 A.2d 405 (1967).

[7] UNIFORM CONSUMER CREDIT CODE, Working Draft # 6, § 2.415 (1967).

transfers it to a financer, such financer might attain the rights of a holder in due course even though he purchased the note knowing it was a consumer note which the seller had taken unlawfully. Professor Murphy, on the other hand, seems to believe that knowledge that the note in question was taken in connection with a consumer-credit sale, and thus unlawfully, will negative the financer's good faith, and that, pursuant to the Uniform Commercial Code,[8] this will prevent him from attaining holder-in-due-course status.

Professor Bailey's general description of the substantive provisions of the Uniform Consumer Credit Code is followed by Professor Spanogle's treatment of the proposed code's enforcement provisions. This treatment is highly critical. While Professor Spanogle agrees with the draftsmen's decision to establish a state "Administrator" to enforce the code in the interest of consumers, he feels that the present draft fails to give the Administrator adequate power. With respect to private remedies available to individual consumers, he is in basic disagreement with the draftsmen. They have opted for rather limited private remedies, at least in part because they recognize the risk that "too great enhancements of debtors' rights or remedies, might deprive the less credit-worthy of lawful sources of credit and drive them to 'loan sharks' and other illegal credit grantors in whose hands they will enjoy no legal protections. . . ."[9] Professor Spanogle believes that the result is a set of ineffective private remedies which are likely to lead to a failure of the code's consumer-protection policies in states that lack strong administrators.

In a lively article Professor Murphy details the increasingly vigorous attack on the affording of holder-in-due-course status to financers of consumer sales. While this assault has attained considerable success in the courts and legislatures of a number of states, others, including Ohio, have continued to allow the purchasers of consumer paper to take free of the consumer's personal defenses. With the promulgation of the Uniform Consumer Credit Code, these recalcitrant states will be confronted with a serious reform effort. Fairness to consumers calls for a positive response. But, as Professor Murphy points out, it does not require the enactment of the code alternative which would completely destroy the efficacy of a waiver-of-defense clause in a consumer note. The less drastic

---

8 UNIFORM COMMERCIAL CODE, §§ 1-201(19), 3-302(1)(c).

9 UNIFORM CONSUMER CREDIT CODE, Working Draft # 6, Prefatory Note at 3 (1967).

alternative, which would allow a purchaser of consumer paper to take free of personal defenses if (1) he was not on notice that he was purchasing from a disreputable merchant and if (2) the consumer did not give him notice of a defense within a given time period,[10] appears adequate to provide fair treatment in the great majority of transactions.

Important as it is, the prospect of legislative reform is of small comfort to the consumer who has already been victimized by an overreaching merchant. Such consumers must rely on existing law —including the Uniform Commercial Code. In more instances than are generally recognized, this provides important avenues of relief. Hence the pertinence of the guide to the sales article of the Code based on Professor Shanker's address. As this points out, sales warranties arise more frequently than one might at first suspect, provisions which purport to negative or limit them are often vulnerable to attack, and the doctrines of fair dealing and unconscionability are of significant potential value to the poor consumer. On a more general level, this article teaches that the poverty lawyer, no less than the corporate lawyer, must be knowledgeable, imaginative and thorough. This of course is true not only with respect to the existing Uniform Commercial Code; it will also be true with respect to all future consumer-oriented legislation.

In the final piece in the symposium, Mr. Merlin Miller, a layman who serves as a consultant to the Cooperative League of the U.S.A., explores the opportunities and difficulties involved in the use of cooperatives as aids to poor consumers. While Mr. Miller does not deal in detail with the strictly legal problems of consumer cooperatives, he nevertheless has important advice for those who would serve as their counsel. As business ventures, such cooperatives must, if they are to be successful, be operated in businesslike fashion, which means in a manner different from that to which their owners, the poor consumers, are accustomed. Hence, the representation of a consumer cooperative will call for a large measure of economic education and leadership as well as sound legal advice. And, as Mr. Miller suggests, such education has a dual importance. Not only is it essential to the success of the cooperative entity, it is also likely to be of independent value to the members of the cooperative. In fact, the indirect educational benefits of cooperative participation may, more often than not, outweigh the direct financial advantages.

---

10 UNIFORM CONSUMER CREDIT CODE, Working Draft # 6, § 2.404 Alternative A (1967).

# THE SUBSTANTIVE PROVISIONS OF THE UNIFORM CONSUMER CREDIT CODE: 20th CENTURY CONSUMER PROTECTION IN A FREE ENTERPRISE SYSTEM

HENRY J. BAILEY III*

## I. AN OVERVIEW OF THE UNIFORM CONSUMER CREDIT CODE

The proposed Uniform Consumer Credit Code has gone through several drafts to date. This article is addressed to the latest version, Working Draft No. 6, dated December 4, 1967. References to the Code or to the "U3C" are to Working Draft No. 6, unless otherwise specified.[1] The U3C itself is the product of the National Conference of Commissioners on Uniform State Laws. It was painstakingly drafted by the Conference[2] and has been subjected to thorough and highly critical review by various members of an advisory committee which consists of representatives of different kinds of lending organizations and representatives of various consumer or public groups.

The U3C is designed to replace a myriad of piecemeal and non-uniform state laws[3] dealing with such consumer credit transactions

---

* Associate Professor of Law, Willamette University.

1 Copies of Working Draft No. 6 of the U3C may be obtained, to the extent available, from the National Conference of Commissioners on Uniform State Laws, 1155 E. 60th St., Chicago, Ill. 60637. See footnote 1 of Prof. Spanogle's article, this issue, for explanation of "U3C" citation.

2 The principal draftsmen have been Professors William D. Warren and Robert L. Jordan, both of the University of California School of Law, Los Angeles (UCLA), and they have been assisted by Professor Robert W. Johnson, School of Industrial Administration, Purdue University. A number of the Commissioners on Uniform State Laws have personally participated in the project, and consultants and researchers have also participated in various capacities.

A public hearing on the U3C was conducted in Chicago on June 16-17, 1967, attended by members of the advisory committee and others. That hearing considered a prior draft of the U3C and consisted of both written memoranda and oral presentations. See Proceedings, Public Hearing on Second Tentative Draft of the Proposed Uniform Consumer Credit Code, which may be obtained from the National Conference on Commissioners on Uniform State Laws, 1155 E. 60th St., Chicago, Ill. 60637. [Hereinafter cited as Proceedings.]

3 For a thorough analysis of existing consumer credit laws as of a few years ago, see CURRAN, TRENDS IN CONSUMER CREDIT LEGISLATION (1965). For a briefer analysis by the same author, see Curran, Legislative Controls as a Response to Consumer-Credit Problems, 8 B.C. IND. & COM. L. REV. 409 (1967).

For some of the background, see Jordan and Warren, A Proposed Uniform Code for Consumer Credit, 8 B.C. IND. & COM. L. REV. 441 (1967). [Hereinafter cited

5   [597]

(and sometimes other credit transactions as well) as retail installment sales,[4] revolving credit agreements or so-called "revolving budget" agreements,[5] small loans,[6] bank installment loans,[7] second mortgage loans,[8] and assignments of wages or earnings,[9] and is further designed to replace the general laws relating to limitations on interest and usury.[10]

The "substantive" provisions dealing with consumer credit sales and leases and consumer loans are found in articles two and three of the U3C.[11] The draftsmen considered it preferable to separate substantive treatment of consumer credit sales (and leases) from that of consumer loans. This accords with the traditional separation of credit sales and loans arising under the time-price doctrine with regard to sales.[12] However, because the provisions of Article 2 on sales and Article 3 on loans are for the most part parallel in coverage and quite similar in language and draftsmanship, it is expedient to consider the two articles together.

---

as Jordan & Warren.] Current news of the consumer credit project is given in virtually every issue of the PERSONAL FINANCE LAW QUARTERLY REPORT.

Texas has varied to some degree from the general trend of enacting piecemeal legislation, by enacting in 1967 a comprehensive statute regulating most consumer credit transactions, including loans of $2,500 or less and most retail installment sales. The language and form of the Texas statutes is rather similar to that found in many of the separated and piecemeal consumer credit statutes found in other states. TEX. REV. CIV. STAT. ANN., art. 5069 (Supp. 1967).

[4] *E.g.*, OHIO REV. CODE ANN. §§ 1317.01-.11 (Page 1962).

[5] *E.g.*, OHIO REV. CODE ANN. § 1317.11 (Page 1962).

[6] *E.g.*, OHIO REV. CODE ANN. §§ 1321.01-.19 (Page 1962).

[7] Loans payable in installments or by means of periodic deposits are permitted on the part of banks under a provision of the new Ohio Banking Code, OHIO REV. CODE ANN. § 1107.26 (Page Supp. 1967). A similar provision of former law applied to "special plan" banks, similar to industrial banks of other states. OHIO REV. CODE ANN. § 1115.10 (Page 1953 now repealed).

Some states have rather extensive installment loan statutes applicable to such loans by banks. *E.g.*, N.Y. BANK. LAW § 108 (McKinney 1950).

[8] *E.g.*, OHIO REV. CODE ANN. §§ 1321.51-.60 (Page Supp. 1967).

[9] *E.g.*, OHIO REV. CODE ANN. §§ 1321.31-.33 (Page 1962).

[10] *E.g.*, OHIO REV. CODE ANN. §§ 1343.01-.05 (Page 1962).

[11] In a manner analogous to .that of the Uniform Commercial Code, the U3C is organized in numbered articles and sections, *i.e.*, "U3C § 2.101."

[12] Under the time-price doctrine, a credit sale may be made at a higher price than that charged for a cash sale of the same item of property, and such price differential is not "interest" within the ambit of the usury law limitations on interest. The time-price doctrine has been the law of most states, including Ohio. *See* 54 OHIO JUR. 2D *Usury* § 13 (1962). Credit sales, however, are subject to retail installment sales statutes, such as OHIO REV. CODE ch. 1317 (Page 1953). *See* Annot., 14 A.L.R.3d 1065 (1967).

## II. Disclosure of Financing Rates

A. *Simple Annual Interest*

The most controversial subject in the entire area of consumer credit has been that relating to required disclosure of the essential terms of a consumer credit transaction in such a manner as to enable a consumer to have some meaningful information as to what he must pay for credit, and thus to enable him to "shop" for credit by comparing the rates of different credit extenders.[13] There are state disclosure statutes of various kinds.[14] At the federal level considerable attention has been directed to legislation that would require written disclosure to the borrower in a consumer credit transaction of the cost of his credit in terms that he should presumably understand. Such disclosure will require that the finance charge be stated as a simple annual percentage rate of interest. The federal Truth in Lending Act[15] contemplates that states will adopt laws requiring disclosure in a manner substantially similar to the federal requirements.[16]

The U3C provisions on disclosure have been drafted to coincide with expected Congressional thinking, and it would seem that ultimately the U3C disclosure provisions[17] must depend on the Congressional action taken. Since most of the Congressional proposals to date had called for disclosure in terms of an annual percentage rate of interest,* that method is followed in the current draft of the U3C.[18]

To cover the credit sale and consumer loan dichotomy, the disclosure provisions are double-jointed. They do not apply to sales "other than sales of interests in land" or to leases,[19] where the

---

[13] See Jordan & Warren, *Disclosure of Finance Charges: A Rationale*, 64 Mich. L. Rev. 1285 (1966); 18 Vand. L. Rev. 856 (1965).

[14] For summary of some state disclosure statutes, see 16 De Paul L. Rev. 464 (1967).

For a decision dealing with the effect of non-disclosure under a state statute, see American Home Improvement, Inc. v. MacIver, 105 N.H. 435, 201 A.2d 886 (1964). See Annot., 14 A.L.R.3d 330 (1967).

[15] 82 Stat. 146 (1968), 1968 *United States Code, Cong. and Admin. News* 1232.

[16] *Id.* at 1245.

[17] U3C § 2.301 *et seq.* apply to credit sales and § 3.301 *et seq.* apply to loans.

[18] See U3C § 2.301 *et seq.* Working Draft No. 4, prepared earlier in 1967, had required disclosure in terms of dollars per one hundred dollars per year.

* This article was in galley proofs when the Truth in Lending Act was enacted. The editors have made some adjustments, but some anachronisms necessarily appear.—Ed.

[19] The general coverage of Article 2 with respect to consumer credit sales and consumer leases is set forth in U3C §§ 2.102, 2.104 and 2.106.

amount involved is 25,000 dollars or more.[20] Similarly, the disclosure provisions do not apply to loans[21] other than those "secured primarily by an interest in land" of 25,000 dollars or more.[22]

For the ordinary consumer installment credit sale or loan, the key requirement is disclosure of the approximate annual percentage rate of the finance charge, where the charge is ten dollars or more,[23] calculated under what is termed in the U3C as the "United States rule."[24] For example, assume that 500 dollars is financed for four months at a total service charge of $12.56. The total balance to be repaid is $512.56 and the monthly payment is $128.14. A monthly interest rate of one percent will satisfy the rule;[25] and that rate would be multiplied by twelve to give an annual rate of twelve percent which must be disclosed.[26] "Approved" tables will likely be compiled for use by credit sellers and lenders which will carry rates expressed in terms of annual percentages for varying amounts and number of installments of credit.[27]

In addition to the annual percentage rate, other elements must also be disclosed in the ordinary consumer credit transaction. Where there is a credit sale, the cash price, the down payment (including trade-in allowance), license fees, official or filing fees, insurance premiums, certain "permitted" additional charges, the credit service charge, the total unpaid balance, and the number of payments, including the amount and due date of each, must be disclosed.[28] These requirements are similar to those of a number of existing retail installment sales statutes.[29] Analogous requirements of itemization and

[20] U3C § 2.301(1).

[21] The general coverage of the disclosure provisions of Article 3 with respect to consumer loans is set forth in U3C §§ 3.302, 3.304, and 3.306.

[22] U3C § 3.301(1).

[23] U3C §§ 2.306(3), 3.306(2)(j).

[24] "United States rule" indicates the actuarial method of allocating payments made on a debt between principal or amount financed and loan finance charge or credit service charge, pursuant to which a payment is applied first to the accumulated loan finance charge or credit service charge and the balance is applied to the unpaid principal or amount financed. U3C § 1.301(15).

[25] Complete mathematical accuracy is not required. A calculation of the rate which will equal the finance charge to the nearest whole dollar is all that is necessary. U3C §§ 2.304(2), 3.304(2).

[26] The example in the comment to U3C § 2.304, while illustrating the proper method, has been garbled by the misplacing of decimal points. The figures there illustrate an annual rate of 120%, not 12% as indicated.

[27] The enforcing agency is empowered to publish guidelines, in the form of tables or otherwise, for determining rates to be disclosed. U3C §§ 2.304(7), 3.304(7).

[28] U3C § 2.306(2).

[29] *See, e.g.,* the present Ohio Retail Installment Sales statute. OHIO REV. CODE ANN. § 1317.04 (Page 1962).

disclosure of the elements of a consumer loan also exist.[30] This, too, has counterparts in existing small loan statutes.[31]

Some additional provisions of the U3C require disclosure where there is refinancing of an existing credit,[32] consolidation of credits,[33] or deferment of one or more due payments.[34] Disclosure is also called for where installment loans are made pursuant to the use of a credit card or similar arrangement[35] and where a consumer lease is entered into which is payable in installments.[36] Disclosure on an estimated basis is permitted, since advance disclosure may at times be impossible.[37] The debtor, however, is entitled to a copy of any writing which he signs.[38] Where a sale or lease is arranged by mail or telephone, the required disclosure may be made within a reasonable time, and before the first installment is due.[39] Where a loan is arranged by mail, disclosure is necessary at the time of reciept of the proceeds of the loan by the debtor.[40] Where the credit is repayable

---

30 U3C § 3.306(2).

31 The present Ohio Small Loans Act requires delivery to the borrower of a statement of the amount and date of the loan, a schedule of payments or a description thereof, the type of security, the name and address of the licensed office of the lending organization and of each borrower, and "the agreed rate of charge," or in lieu thereof, a copy of all obligations signed by the borrower. A copy of a lengthy statutory provision is also required to be furnished to the borrower. OHIO REV. CODE ANN. § 1321.14(A) (Page 1962). Apparently, all borrowers are assumed to be able to read and understand the wording of lengthy statutes, at least as well as law students. Somewhat similar requirements exist with respect to certain second mortgage loans in Ohio. See OHIO REV. CODE ANN. § 1321.58 (Page Supp. 1967).

32 U3C § 2.307.

33 U3C §§ 2.308, 3.307. This refers to consolidation of the amount owed on a previous credit sale or loan with a current credit sale or additional loan. See U3C §§ 2.206, 3.206.

34 U3C §§ 2.309, 3.308.

35 U3C § 3.310, which requires basic disclosure of the rate and additional charges before a credit card installment loan is made and which then refers to U3C § 3.306 for other disclosure requirements similar to those for other installment loans after a credit card loan is made. This does not apply to revolving credits.

36 U3C § 2.311 contains no requirement of disclosure of an annual percentage rate, since there is no "interest" normally connected with a lease. This raises, however, the question whether credit sales can be disguised as installment leases by those who desire to avoid disclosure on the basis of an annual percentage rate.

37 U3C §§ 2.302(4), 3.302(4), which permit disclosure of estimates of the required information with an indication that such are estimates where "it is not commercially feasible" to give the exact information.

38 U3C §§ 2.302(5), 3.302(5).

39 U3C § 2.305.

40 U3C § 3.305, which, perhaps on the assumption that no loans are ever made by telephone, makes no provision for such loans. It might also be noted that no provision

in installments, but one of the installments is not equal to the others, or where the due date of the first payment is not equal to the interval between installment payments, or where provision is made for dispensing with an installment payment in any one or more payment periods, disclosure of the rate may be made as if the debt is payable under an agreement having the same amount or principal, the same term or maturity, and "a regular schedule of payments having the same interval between payments as under the actual contract."[41]

The U3C also restricts to some extent the content of advertising in connection with consumer credits. False advertising concerning the terms and conditions of a credit or loan is prohibited.[42] In general, advertising of consumer credit transactions need not follow the "disclosure" requirements; however, if credit or loan advertising states the rate or dollar amount of credit or finance charge or the amount of installment payments, then the advertisement must disclose the rate in terms of a simple annual percentage.[43] Guidelines as to the kinds of advertising permitted may be issued by supervisory authorities.[44]

## B. *Disclosure Where There Is A Revolving Credit*

Where a credit of fixed amount is extended on a set date for a definite term repayable in equal installments of equal amounts during equal intervals of time, the terms of the credit are predictable. Even to calculate a simple annual interest rate in percentage for such a predictable credit requires a degree of mathematical wizardry beyond the ken of the average individual, including the average attorney, law student, or law faculty member. However, the use of tables will probably make it possible even for sales or clerical personnel of credit sellers or installment lenders to compute for each loan the simple annual percentage rate that must be disclosed. In any event, such credits consist of constants which make computation of an annual percentage rate possible at the inception of the credit.

On the other hand, where a revolving credit is created under

---

is made for cases where the proceeds of a loan are not directly advanced to the debtor but are used to pay a third person, such as a seller, the fact situation of Ohio Loan & Discount Co. v. Tyarks, 173 Ohio St. 564, 184 N.E.2d 374 (1962).

41 U3C §§ 2.304(3), 3.304(3), which in effect permit disclosure of such "irregular" loans as if they were for the same total term and same amount but repayable in substantially equal payments over equal periods of time.

42 U3C §§ 2.303(1), 3.303(1) which might be said generally to "prohibit sin."

43 U3C §§ 2.303(2), 3.303(2). Some exemption exists for charges of $10 or less.

44 U3C §§ 2.303(3), 3.303(3).

a credit card, charge account, or check loan or overdraft by a bank, variables exist which make it impossible to compute an accurate rate on an annual percentage basis. In the typical revolving credit situation, there may be no service or finance charge where payment is made within a fixed period, such as thirty days after the date the bill is sent.[45] After such period a service or finance charge might be computed at a certain rate, such as one and a half percent per month, on the average unpaid balance during the next month or on the unpaid balance as of a certain date in the next month. The actual rate measured on a monthly or annual percentage basis will increase or decrease because of such variables as the time and amount of new purchases or credit extensions or the time and amounts of payments made.

The draftsmen of the U3C recognized the practical impossibility of making accurate advance disclosure in a revolving credit situation on the basis of a simple annual percentage rate; they merely required disclosure at the time the account is opened of the conditions under which a service or finance charge is to be made, the method of computation, and description of any additional charges made. In the usual revolving credit situation this must be stated as a percentage and the equivalent annual rate must be given.[46] Certain information must be given at each monthly billing including the same information as to rates as is required at the inception of the arrangement.[47] Although revolving charge account sales and revolving loan transactions are separately treated with respect to disclosure requirements,[48] the treatment is so similar as to be identical for all practical purposes. In fact, if a person makes both revolving credit sales and revolving credit loans, he may treat all transactions the same and need give only a single statement at the time any statement is required.[49]

---

45 For example, a purchase may be made on December 1, the billing may be made as of January 2; payment in full received by February 1 will excuse any service or finance charge. Thus virtually two months of free credit are possible. On the other hand, another purchase may be made on December 31, which is caught in the same January bill. Only one month of free credit exists as to this second purchase.

46 U3C §§ 2.310(1), 3.309(1). For example, if a charge is made at the rate of 1½ percent of the average daily balance in the account for the month, exclusive of purchases made that month (a typical revolving charge account arrangement) such must be disclosed and the equivalent annual percentage rate of 18% must be stated.

47 U3C §§ 2.310(2), 3.309(2).

48 U3C § 2.310 (revolving credit sales or sales pursuant to revolving charge accounts); U3C § 3.309 (revolving loan accounts).

49 U3C §§ 2.310(3), 3.309(3). An example where one person might be both a seller on revolving credit and a revolving credit lender might arise where a particular credit

In summary, disclosure in connection with a revolving credit is sufficient if it merely states the conditions under which a charge is made and the monthly rate and basis multiplied by twelve. It is not necessary for the credit extender to be a fortune-teller and estimate the rate based on actual charges incurred and payments made.

> It is irony indeed that during the decade in which adherents of 'truth-in-lending' legislation fought so valiantly for its passage, the only sales transaction in which disclosure on an annual interest basis can be made with accuracy—the closed-end install-ment sale—was greatly diminishing in importance in all but high-price transactions like the sale of automobiles. This was due to the rapid growth of revolving credit, and if this trend continues, 'truth-in-lending' legislation may well offer a solu-tion to a problem that has largely disappeared.[50]

## C. *Disclosure: Does The U3C Do The Job?*

The disclosure requirements of the U3C must, of necessity, con-form with those of any federal enactment, but the provisions pro-posed in the current draft of the U3C are ones with which a legiti-mate lender or credit seller can live.[51] The U3C draftsmen appear to have been more realistic than certain elected public servants in not expecting the impossible or the extremely impracticable in con-nection with "truth in lending." It is hoped that no ultimate Con-gressional enactment on the subject will be so politically motivated as to ignore the realities and force into an unacceptable mold any state legislation dealing with disclosure.

A few comments might be in order. First, U3C disclosure re-quirements, unlike those of some prior statutes, do not prescribe exact formats in sales or loan contracts, such as signatures, size of type, notice to the buyer or borrower, and the like.[52] Since there are many kinds of credit sellers, some statutory format might perhaps be desirable. This might be covered by a comment, when comments

---

card issued by a selling organization is used both to charge sales of products of that company through its own outlets and sales by independents, who write up charge sales and turn them over to the company, which bills the customer directly. *See* Jordan & Warren, *supra* note 3, at 446.

50 Jordan & Warren, *supra* note 3, at 446-47.

51 This presupposes that the purpose of any consumer credit legislation is to regulate reasonably and not to "kill the goose that laid the golden eggs," thus making loan sharks the sole source of consumer credit.

52 For example, the "Unruh Act" dealing with retail installment sales in Cali-fornia has a number of requirements as to provisions and sometimes exact wording to be included in a retail installment sales contract and, in some instances the size of type to be used. *See* CALIF. CIV. CODE ch. 1803 (West Supp. 1967).

are finally drafted. The great majority of sellers and lenders who desire to obey the law might find such guidance helpful. It might also be desirable to require disclosure of any balloon payment (where permitted) in some conspicuous manner. Furthermore, although it is probably impracticable to forbid blanks completely, some form of statutory protection for the consumer or borrower who signs a blank contract or obligation might be desirable.[53]

## III. RATE LIMITATIONS

### A. *Rate Ceilings and Usury*

The U3C makes some fundamental changes in the general law with respect to credit ceilings or maximum rates. It does away with general usury laws which limit the "contract" rate[54] charge for the use of money.[55] This is justified on the following grounds:

> . . . [U]sury laws imposing inflexible price ceilings on money and credit are historical vestiges of the supposition that emperors, kings and governments could effectively fix all prices; the need to escape the rigidity of usury laws has led to special laws, which only the expert can find or understand, for each type of credit transaction requiring a charge higher than the usury rate.[56]

The U3C might have been drafted as an exception to the general usury laws, thus permitting higher rates with respect to consumer credit while leaving the general usury laws operative in areas of non-consumer credit.[57] For a number of reasons, such an ap-

---

53 Suggestions here are difficult, but it might be provided that a copy of the completed contract be furnished the debtor promptly upon completion, and that the debtor be given a period in which to question the accuracy of the completion and possibly to rescind the transaction if the completed form does not conform with the debtor's understanding. For examples of what might be possible see U3C §§ 2.501-.505 on home solicitation sales.

54 Existing state usury laws set a "legal" or "judgment" rate of interest when the rate is not otherwise stipulated and a "contract" rate, which is the highest rate that may be charged by agreement of the parties. In many states the permitted "contract" rate is higher than the "legal" rate. The intent of the U3C draftsmen is to do away with general "contract" rate limitations, although preserving "legal" or "judgment" rates. In Ohio, the "contract" rate is 8 percent; the "legal" rate is 6 percent. OHIO REV. CODE ANN. §§ 1343.01 (contract rate) and 1343.03 (legal rate) (Page 1962).

55 U3C §§ 2.605 and 3.605 expressly permit the parties to agree in writing to any service charge in the case of credit sales or loans which are not subject to the various ceilings or protective provisions of the U3C. In addition, U3C § 9.102 expressly calls for the repeal of laws relating to usury in general.

56 Prefatory Note to Working Draft No. 6, U3C, at 2 (1967).

57 This is similar to the present statutory scheme of many states whereby there

proach was not followed. It is more in keeping with our economic development to limit rate ceilings only on those loans which need limitation, leaving it to "free enterprise" to limit rates on such loans as those of large amounts made to business organizations.[58] Furthermore, general usury laws have often failed to protect consumer credit sale transactions because of the time-price doctrine, which holds that a sale in a free market on credit might be made at a higher price than a cash sale and that such a higher credit price is not a loan of money.[59] Moreover, there is at least a slight possibility that the statutory combination of a general usury law and special higher rates for certain kinds of loans or credit transactions might run into state constitutional difficulties.[60] In any event the maximum limits of general usury laws are too low to afford any practical protection to the consumer.[61] In fact, general usury laws in many states have the sole effect of setting rate ceilings on commercial-type loans, as to which price-control protection is hardly needed. Finally, although general usury laws ordinarily carry maximum rates too low to give adequate protection at a realistic level, such general usury laws may present an unexpected trap to unwary lenders in commercial credit transactions.[62] Although abolition of general usury rate limitations will seem to many to be a radical change in the law and thus subject to

---

is a general usury law setting a maximum contract rate, accompanied by certain exemptions, such as that for loans to corporations, and also accompanied by higher rates with respect to consumer credit transactions.

[58] This is the statutory scheme in Maine, Massachusetts, and New Hampshire, which have no general usury laws, although certain credit transactions such as consumer credits are regulated. The other states have "contract" rate limitations ranging from 6 percent in New York and some other states to 21 percent in Rhode Island. The rate limitation in Ohio is 8 percent. OHIO REV. CODE ANN. § 1343.01 (Page 1962).

[59] *See, e.g.*, Theodore Roosevelt Agency, Inc. v. General Motors Acceptance Corp., 156 Colo. 237, 398 P.2d 965 (1965) and Lundstrom v. Radio Corp. of America, 17 Utah 2d 114, 405 P.2d 339 (1965). *See* 14 A.L.R.3d 1058 (1967).

[60] Such a problem arose in Nebraska a few years ago under a state constitutional provision prohibiting "special laws" fixing interest rates, in Elder v. Doerr, 175 Neb. 483, 122 N.W.2d 528 (1963), *petition for cert. dismissed*, 377 U.S. 973 (1964). It is not likely, however, to arise in Ohio which lacks a similar constitutional provision.

[61] Legitimate consumer lenders could not operate profitably while making consumer installment loans at rates permitted by general usury laws. *See* Curran, *Legislative Controls as a Response to Consumer-Credit Problems*, 8 B.C. IND. & COM. L. REV. 409, 411 (1967) which points out that this inability to operate profitably brought about the Uniform Small Loan Law of the Russell Sage Foundation which now exists in some form in many states.

[62] *See, e.g.*, Hollamon v. First State Bank, 389 P.2d 352 (Okla. 1963). In that case a bank loan of $20,000, repayable in 23 monthly installments of $1,000 each, was held to exceed the 10 percent per year usury limit.

condemnation, this writer finds the preferable approach is to do away with all existing rate ceilings and make a new start with the realistic rate ceilings of a uniform consumer credit code.[63]

In practice, not too many loans are freed from the statutory rate ceilings by the suggested repeal of general usury laws. The U3C sets rate ceilings for consumer credit transactions. Furthermore, there are rate ceilings covering non-consumer credit extensions to individuals in the amount of 25,000 dollars or less. Most corporate credits and all credits over 25,000 dollars, however, are freed of rate ceilings.[64]

## B.  *Specific Rate Limitations*

Another unusual approach taken in the U3C with respect to maximum rates is to set rate ceilings that are rather high, often much higher than those under statutes which the U3C will replace. The draftsmen here recognized the risk that

> too low ceiling rates, too substantial restrictions on creditors' rights and remedies, or too great enhancements of debtors' rights or remedies, might deprive the less credit-worthy of lawful sources of credit and drive them to "loan sharks" and other illegal credit grantors in whose hands they will enjoy no legal protections.[65]

In short, the setting of restrictively low ceiling rates would merely deny credit extension by any reputable organization to the marginal borrower and relegate such borrower to those who operate illegally.[66] High maximum rates are also justified on the ground that a maximum ceiling on a credit sale is of limited utility, since the seller can exceed the ceiling by merely raising the price of the articles sold.[67]

---

[63] There will be an added problem in a few states where the usury limitations are embodied in state constitutions. Arkansas illustrates the extreme rigidity in this regard with its constitutional ceiling of 10 percent per year. ARK. CONST., art. 19, § 13.

[64] A person who can borrow over $25,000 is probably "sophisticated" enough to bargain for reasonably favorable rates. In practice, the rates on such larger loans should rarely come close to the 18 percent figure limiting individual nonconsumer loans of $25,000 or less.

[65] Prefatory Note to Working Draft No. 6, U3C, at 3 (1967) which also points out that it was the "loan shark" evil that the Russell Sage Foundation proposed to remedy with its Uniform Small Loan Law.

[66] There are no penal provisions in the U3C directed at loan sharks. Such lenders are already subject to the penalties of prohibitory statutes in many jurisdictions. The U3C approach is to make rates high enough so that reputable lenders may operate. This should result in legitimate lenders charging rates that are considerably lower than those charged by illegal operators.

[67] Jordan & Warren, *supra* note 3, at 451. The authors, who are also the principal

The rate limitations for consumer credit sales and consumer loans are set forth currently in two alternatives. The first permits eighteen dollars per 100 dollars per year on the first 300 dollars, twelve dollars per 100 dollars per year on the amount from 300 dollars to 1,000 dollars and eight dollars per 100 dollars per year on amounts over 1,000 dollars. The second permits percentages per year on unpaid balances of thirty-six percent on the first 300 dollars, twenty-one percent on the amount from 300 dollars to 1,000 dollars, and fifteen percent on the amount over 1,000 dollars. In lieu of either alternative, a flat eighteen percent per year on the unpaid balance is also permitted.[68] In the case of a revolving credit, the maximum rate may not exceed two percent per month on the amount outstanding[69] which is 500 dollars or less and one and a half percent on that part of the amount over 500 dollars.[70]

The maximum rates apply to all consumer credits, regardless of the identity of the lender. In other words, the U3C does not (like some prior statutes) set one rate for small loan companies or personal finance companies, another rate for banks making installment loans, still another rate for retail installment sales, and perhaps varying rates for retail installment sales of motor vehicles dependent upon the model year of the vehicle. In any instance, however, where rates are filed with and approved by a subdivision or agency of the enacting state or of the United States, the rate ceilings of the U3C do not apply.[71]

Additional charges permitted include official fees, charges for insurance, and "reasonable" charges "for other benefits conferred upon" the debtor.[72] In the case of a loan, a permitted additional

---

draftsmen of the U3C, point out that this would cause the cash buyer to pay part of the credit charge in lieu of the credit buyer.

[68] U3C §§ 2.201(2), 3.508(2) (drafted in alternatives). The flat 18 percent alternative rate is computed under the United States rule.

[69] A formula is given for calculating the amount outstanding in U3C §§ 2.207(2), 3.509(2) to cover fluctuating amounts resulting from additional charges incurred during the billing period or payments received during the billing period. The amount may be computed on the average daily balance, the balance as of a certain day each month, or the "median" amount.

[70] U3C §§ 2.207(3), 3.509(3). Where the billing cycle is other than monthly, there is provision for a statutory translation into monthly terms.

[71] U3C §§ 2.211, 3.207. An example might be loans for home improvement guaranteed by the Federal Housing Administration, which may be made at rates permitted by that agency.

[72] U3C §§ 2.202, 3.202.

The provision for "reasonable" charges "for other benefits conferred upon" the debtor is rather indefinite and might open the door to abuse. What is probably con-

charge may include an annual fee for the privilege of using a credit card, as where the credit card may be used in widespread purchases.[73]

The provision on additional charges may be criticized for incompleteness. Some prior consumer credit statutes have spelled out in more detail what additional charges are permissible.[74] In general, it seems that additional charges are permitted by the U3C for any necessary and legitimate payments which are made to third persons. Examples include insurance premiums, filing fees, and the like. Some closing fees, if reasonable and related to actual handling expenses, might also be separately collected.[75]

Other charges permitted include delinquency charges,[76] charges where one or more payments are deferred,[77] charges where a credit is refinanced,[78] and charges permitted where a new credit sale or loan is consolidated with a prior credit sale or loan.[79] A charge may also be made where the creditor makes an advance to perform certain duties normally required of the buyer, such as insuring or preserving the collateral.[80]

The U3C gives the buyer the right to prepay in full any consumer credit without penalty.[81] Upon such prepayment in full, a rebate is required under the familiar "rule of seventy-eights."[82]

---

templated here are charges for possible benefits or services given the debtor, such as a charge per check drawn in a check loan, or possible service or closing charges. Abuse in this area might be limited by a provision permitting the state official charged with enforcement of the U3C to adopt rules as to additional charges. U3C §§ 2.202(2), 3.202(2).

[73] U3C § 3.202(1)(c). There is no equivalent in connection with credit sales.

[74] This is not so in Ohio. The chief additional charge permitted in a retail installment sales contract is a "service charge" dependent on the term of the credit and the principal balance. OHIO REV. CODE ANN. § 1317.06(A)(2) (Page 1962). A separate charge for insurance is also permitted. OHIO REV. CODE ANN. §§ 1317.04(D), 1317.05 (Page 1962). For charges in connection with small loans, see OHIO REV. CODE ANN. § 1321.13 (Page 1962).

[75] Abuses are possible in connection with excessive closing fees and also in connection with such matters as broker's or finder's fees.

[76] U3C §§ 2.203, 3.203.

[77] U3C §§ 2.204, 3.204.

[78] U3C §§ 2.205, 3.205.

[79] U3C §§ 2.206, 3.206.

[80] U3C §§ 2.208, 3.208.

[81] U3C §§ 2.209, 3.209. The Comment points out that there is no right to prepay a sale of an interest in real property or to make a partial prepayment.

[82] U3C §§ 2.210, 3.210. A somewhat similar rule exists in connection with retail installment sales in Ohio. OHIO REV. CODE ANN. § 1317.09 (Page 1962).

## C. *Rate Ceilings for Non-Consumer Credit*

Although the repeal of general usury laws is contemplated, some non-consumer credit sale and loan transactions are also subjected to rate ceilings. These consist of credits of 25,000 dollars or less where the debtor is an individual, or where the debtor is an organization and the debt is secured primarily by a security interest in a one or two family dwelling occupied by a person related to the organization.[83] In addition, when a credit sale is involved, the special non-consumer ceiling governs where " . . . the credit is granted by a seller who regularly engages in credit transactions as a seller."[84] There is no ceiling on loans or credit sales over 25,000 dollars. There is also no ceiling on non-consumer sales by a person not in the business of selling on credit or on non-consumer credits to corporations or other organizations, except where a one or two-family dwelling is used as security.

Non-consumer credits which are subject to rate ceilings are governed by a ceiling of eighteen percent per year on unpaid balances. In other words, there is a "partial usury law" of eighteen percent on many non-consumer credit transactions.[85] However, the parties may agree to subject any non-consumer credit transaction to the provisions of the U3C applicable to consumer credit transactions,[86] including the rate ceilings previously discussed, which often may exceed eighteen percent.

Revolving credit transactions in the non-consumer category discussed here are subject to the same maximum rates as consumer revolving credits.[87] A special provision of the U3C exempts any consumer loan with a rate of ten percent per year or less on unpaid balances, which is not a revolving credit loan.[88]

---

[83] U3C §§ 2.602(1), 3.602(1). This sort of requirement would curb the abuse that occasionally has existed where a loan is made on a dwelling house at excessive rates and the lender requires the debtor to incorporate, as a condition to receiving the loan, so that rates in excess of usury ceilings may be charged. *See* Jenkins v. Moyse, 254 N.Y. 319, 172 N.E. 521 (1930). U3C § 1.301(12). defines the term "person related to" with respect to an organization.

[84] U3C § 2.602(1)(a). This would subject to non-consumer ceilings such sales as agricultural equipment to a farmer, an automobile to a doctor for professional use, and the like, if under $25,000.

[85] U3C §§ 2.602(2), 3.602(2).

[86] U3C §§ 2.601, 3.601.

[87] U3C §§ 2.602(3), 3.602(3).

[88] U3C § 3.201.

## D.  *Summary of Rate Limitations*

The U3C sets rather high maximum rates on consumer credit transactions, both sales and loans. In addition, certain other credit transactions while not subject to other provisions of the U3C, such as those dealing with disclosure, are subject to the rate limitations. The intent is to cover in one group of statutes all credit transactions that should be subjected to rate ceilings in order to prevent abuse by unscrupulous lenders. On the other hand, rate ceilings are eliminated with respect to such loans as large business loans on the theory that the rates are, and should be, governed by forces of normal competition among lenders. This realistic reappraisal of rate ceilings is a most salutary reform and should of itself justify widespread enactment of the U3C.

## IV.  Licensing and "Notification" Requirements

A basic tenet of those involved in drafting the U3C is that competition should effectively determine the pricing of money and credit. One means of furthering competition in the credit granting field is to permit credit grantors ". . . relatively easy entry into the market to avoid monopoly."[89] This approach is carried out in the U3C by not requiring the licensing of credit sellers or sales financing companies.[90] Moreover, although the U3C follows the approach of prior statutes[91] in requiring the licensing of companies making so-called "regulated" loans,[92] there are no restrictions on the number of entrants into this field. In other words, there is no "convenience

---

89 Prefatory Note to Working Draft No. 6, U3C, at 2.

90 The Ohio Retail Installment Sales Act also has no licensing provisions for sales finance companies. Ohio Rev. Code Ann. §§ 1317.01-.99 (Page 1962). On the other hand, some states require licensing of those involved in retail installment sales. For example, Florida requires an annual license for a retail installment seller, Fla. Stat. Ann. § 520.32(2) (Supp. 1968), and also for a sales finance company, Fla. Stat. Ann. § 520.52 (Supp. 1968). For some other statutes requiring licensing of sales finance companies, see Ill. Ann. Stat. ch. 121½ § 403 (Smith-Hurd Supp. 1967); N.Y. Bank. Law ch. 492 (McKinney Supp. 1967). Banks and other financial organizations chartered and regulated under other statutes are generally exempt from licensing requirements applicable to sales finance companies.

91 Many states have "small loan" laws, often derived from the Uniform Small Loan Law devised many years ago by the Russell Sage Foundation, which among other matters requires licensing of small loan companies. Ohio requires that small loan companies be licensed. Ohio Rev. Code Ann. §§ 321.02-.44 (Page 1962).

92 U3C §§ 3.501-.507.

and advantage" test as a condition to the issuance of a license.[93] The stated purpose of the U3C licensing requirement is to facilitate entry into the cash-loan field so that the resultant rate competition fostered by disclosure will generally force rates below the permitted maximum charges, with a secondary purpose of reducing the likelihood of localized monopolies in the granting of credit, which would tend to push rates to the maximum permitted levels.[94] There is also no restriction on the carrying on by a loan licensee of some other business ". . . unless he carries on the business for the purpose of evasion or violation of this Act."[95]

In other respects, the licensing provisions applicable to those who make consumer loans are not unlike those of many prior small loan statutes. It is provided that no one may make a "regulated" loan, that is, a consumer loan, pursuant to a revolving credit account or a consumer loan at a rate over ten percent per year on unpaid balances[96] without a license unless the lender is a bank, savings and loan association, credit union, or other financial organization of similar nature, chartered under state or federal law and authorized by such law to make loans and receive deposits, savings or the like.[97]

Provision is made for application for a license,[98] revocation or suspension of a license,[99] the keeping of books and records by licensees,[100] and examination or investigation of licensees by the supervisory authority.[101] It is also provided that administrative action taken by the supervisory authority is to be governed by the state administrative procedure act.[102]

The U3C licensing provisions are similar to, but much simpler than, those of the small loan statutes which are to be replaced. They apply to any consumer lender other than banks, savings and loan associations, credit unions, and the like. They would thus apply in

---

[93] The basic licensing provision, U3C § 3.503, requires only a finding of ". . . financial responsibility, character and fitness." OHIO REV. CODE ANN. § 1321.04(B) (Page 1962), provides that a license may be granted if the Division of Securities finds that allowing the applicant for a license "to engage in such business will promote the convenience and advantage of the community in which the licensed office is to be located."

[94] U3C § 3.503, Comment.

[95] U3C § 3.514.

[96] *See* U3C § 3.501, which defines "regulated loan."

[97] U3C § 3.502, which refers to U3C § 1.301(14).

[98] U3C § 3.503.

[99] U3C § 3.504.

[100] U3C § 3.505.

[101] U3C § 3.506.

[102] U3C § 3.507.

some instances to lending organizations which are now governed by different statutes in the same state.[103]

While a person making consumer credit sales or consumer leases is not required to obtain a license, such a person is required to file a notification with the supervisory authority[104] and, if the credit seller is a nonresident of the state or unqualified out-of-state corporation,[105] to appoint an agent for the service of process. Such requirements apply also to consumer lenders (including those required to be licensed) and to ". . . persons taking assignments or obligations arising from [consumer] sales, leases, or loans, other than assignments in bulk as security for loans."[106] A notification fee must be paid by all persons who are required to file notification. The amount of the fee is based on the volume of credit outstanding.[107]

In general, the U3C licensing provisions are commendable. The approach of dispensing with licensing in connection with sales financing, of simplifying license requirements for lenders, and of permitting entry into the consumer loan field on a purely competitive basis is preferable to the burdensome and often useless requirements of many prior statutes that seem primarily to raise the cost of doing business and thus the cost of consumer credit. It is suggested, however, that the licensing and notification requirements overlap with respect to consumer lenders who make "regulated" loans; therefore, it might be desirable to have the licensing process serve as notification, and to have the notification fees paid by licensees. This would presumably defray the expenses of supervision and examination of licensees,[108] thus forcing credit users, rather than taxpayers in general, to bear the expenses of enforcing the U3C.[109]

---

103 Examples are three kinds of lenders in California governed by different statutes, such as personal property brokers, governed by CAL. FIN. CODE § 22000 (West 1968); small loan companies, governed by CAL. FIN. CODE § 24000 (West 1968); industrial loan companies, governed by CAL. FIN. CODE § 18000 (West 1968). Pennsylvania also has several kinds of lenders: small loan companies, governed by PA. STAT. ANN. tit. 7 § 6151 (1967), and consumer discount companies, governed by PA. STAT. ANN. tit. 7 § 6201 (1967).

104 U3C § 6.202.

105 U3C § 6.203.

106 U3C § 6.201.

107 U3C § 6.204.

108 This is not a suggestion that sales finance companies or the like should be licensed.

109 This is probably the situation with respect to most existing consumer credit statutes. It might also be noted that such supervised financial institutions as banks,

## V. Contract Limitations

### A. *Contract Requirements and Prohibitions*

The U3C confers a number of rights and benefits upon the consumer which may not be waived or may be waived only after default.[110] Certain limitations on agreements and practices are applied to sales involving less than 25,000 dollars credit, leases for less than 25,000 dollars, or loans of less than 25,000 dollars, but not to real estate sales.[111] This avoids the imposition of contract terms that unduly favor the creditor or burden the debtor, which may arise in the smaller credit transactions because of unequal bargaining power or the use of standard-form contracts or contracts of adhesion. The U3C contains a number of protective provisions intended to relieve the consumer from the effects of a hard bargain.[112]

### B. *Home Solicitation Sales*

The purpose of the U3C is to regulate credit, not to regulate sales practices, quality of products sold, misleading advertisements, or other non-credit matters; however, the U3C spills over to regulate a type of sale often associated with credit which has caused particular abuses. This is the "home solicitation sale."[113] Such sales often involve a representative of a credit-selling organization who calls on a family at home and through high pressure salesmanship induces the purchase of grossly overpriced goods.[114] The U3C approaches the problem of such sales[115] by giving the buyer the right to cancel up to

savings and loan associations, credit unions, and the like bear the expenses of examination and other supervision in virtually all states.

110 U3C § 1.107.

111 U3C §§ 2.401, 3.401.

112 Jordan & Warren, *supra* note 3, at 455.

113 A lengthy discussion which highlights many of the abuses in home solicitation sales, particularly where coupled with so-called "referral" plans, is found in State v. ITM, Inc., 52 Misc. 2d 39, 275 N.Y.S.2d 303 (1966), an action by the New York Attorney General to enjoin certain practices deemed "fraudulent and illegal."

114 *See, e.g.,* Frostifresh Corp. v. Reynoso, 54 Misc. 2d 119, 281 N.Y.S.2d 964 (App. Div. 1967), where a refrigerator-freezer was sold under such conditions to a person of Spanish-speaking background, with the sales contract written in English. The facts are given in a lower court opinion in the same case, 52 Misc. 2d 26, 274 N.Y.S.2d 757 (Dist. Ct. 1966).

115 The U3C definition of "home solicitation sale" contemplates a consumer credit sale, payable in installments, of goods or services, where the solicitation is made and the purchase order or offer is given "at a place other than a place of business of the seller." Sales under revolving charge accounts or other sales completed at a permanent store or similar establishment are exempted. Sales arising from solicitations by mail or telephone are probably not included, although this matter might be clarified.

midnight of the third day after the buyer signs the order, by giving written notice to the seller at the address stated in the order.[116] Such notice may be given by mail and is deemed given at the time sent.[117] The agreement in a home solicitation sale must be signed by the buyer, must state the seller's address and must contain a prescribed form of notice of the buyer's right to cancel.[118] Failure to comply with these requirements gives the buyer the absolute right to cancel until such time as there has been compliance.[119] Where the buyer cancels, the seller may retain a fixed amount as a cancellation fee.[120] Within ten days after cancellation the seller must tender to the buyer any payments made, any note or evidence of indebtness given, and any goods traded in or an amount equal to the trade-in allowance given.[121] The buyer has a lien on goods delivered under the cancelled contract to insure return of these items,[122] but on demand by the seller he must make such goods available. If the seller does not make such demand within a reasonable period (presumably forty days) the buyer may keep such goods without payment. While the goods remain in the buyer's possession, he has the duty only to use reasonable care toward them. The seller is entitled to no compensation other than the cancellation fee for services performed prior to cancellation.[123]

The net effect of the "home solicitation sales" provisions is a three day delay in the binding effect of such sales and an option in the buyer to back out during that period without penalty, except the cancellation fee. While some might criticize these provisions as not directly relevant to consumer credit, but rather as aimed at "sharp" sales practices, they do succeed in correcting a substantial evil and for that reason are desirable. Possibly the waiting period might be somewhat longer, such as one week.

## C. *Non-Negotiable Instruments*

One of the major abuses in credit sales comes from the use of negotiable notes. In many instances such a note is executed in favor

---

116 U3C § 2.502(1)(2). Any expression of intent not to be bound is sufficient notice of cancellation. U3C § 2.502(4).

117 U3C § 2.502(3), which requires deposit in a mailbox, with proper address and postage prepaid.

118 U3C § 2.503(1), (2).

119 U3C § 2.503(3).

120 U3C § 2.504(3).

121 U3C § 2.504(1), (2).

122 U3C § 2.504(4).

123 U3C § 2.505, which also provides that the seller must restore to its original condition any property of the buyer which he has altered.

of the seller, together with a conditional sale contract or other security agreement. The buyer may well be under the impression that he can refuse to pay installments which are due if the purchased goods are defective or if there is other absence or failure of consideration. Such a buyer will often find that he is compelled to deal with a third party such as a bank or finance company, with which he did not contemplate any relationship. If the third party has avoided too close a relationship with the seller,[124] and has remained ignorant of the circumstances of the sale,[125] he may be a holder in due course,[126] against whom the buyer has no defense.[127]

The U3C deals with this problem by flatly prohibiting the use of negotiable notes in consumer sales or consumer lease transactions other than those primarily for an agricultural purpose. A negotiable note issued in violation of the U3C provision may nevertheless be enforced by a holder in due course.[128] To be really effective this provision should not only prohibit a seller of consumer credit from using a negotiable note, but also should bar any other person taking a note with knowledge that it was issued in a consumer credit transaction from attaining holder in due course status. Subsequent takers,

---

[124] Too close a business relationship between the finance company and the seller has resulted in a denial of holder in due course status to the finance company. *See* Mutual Finance Co. v. Martin, 63 So. 2d 649 (Fla. 1953). For a particularly flagrant situation where due course holding was denied, see Unico v. Owen, 50 N.J. 101, 232 A.2d 405 (1967).

[125] *See* Lundstrom v. Radio Corp. of America, 17 Utah 2d 114, 405 P.2d 339 (1965). For an example of "too much knowledge," see Norman v. World Wide Distrib., Inc., 202 Pa. Super. 53, 195 A.2d 115 (1963).

[126] UNIFORM COMMERCIAL CODE § 3-302.

[127] A recent example in a case arising under the Uniform Commercial Code is Burchett v. Allied Concord Financial Corp., 74 N.M. 575, 396 P.2d 186 (1964), where the court would not permit the buyer to assert a "personal" defense against a finance company which had taken his note and consumer obligation as holder in due course.

In Ohio, a finance company or other third person that has taken a note, together with a chattel mortgage, conditional sale agreement, or other security agreement, has not been denied holder in due course status merely by reason of such facts alone. Dennis v. Rotter, 43 Ohio App. 330, 183 N.E. 188 (1932). *See generally* 40 OHIO JUR. 2d *Negotiable Instruments* §§ 353, 362; 48 OHIO JUR. 2d *Secured Transactions* § 131. *But cf.* David v. Commercial Credit Corp., 87 Ohio App. 311, 94 N.E.2d 710 (1950), where holder in due course status was denied a finance company which had worked closely with a seller of asbestos siding for dwelling houses, and was, because of its relationship with the seller and knowledge of seller's inferior work for others, charged with knowledge of the seller's inferior work in the particular instance.

For general discussion, see Annot., 44 A.L.R.2d 8 (1955).

[128] U3C § 2.403.

however, such as banks that rediscount paper without dealing with the seller, might be permitted to qualify as holders in due course.[129]

The provision might be improved by broadening its prohibition to include all negotiable instruments, rather than just notes.[130] Moreover, the language designating the rights of a holder in due course might be clarified by specifying that any person taking an instrument with knowledge that it was issued in a consumer credit sale or lease transaction, other than a sale or lease for an agricultural purpose, is barred from holder in due course status. This would make it impossible for anyone who takes a note and separate agreement referring to a consumer credit sale or lease to qualify as a holder in due course. Only one taking a note separated from the agreement might so qualify.[131] Nonetheless, the provision is a desirable one and should provide substantial protection to consumers by preventing many of the abuses which now exist.

The U3C does not bar the use of a negotiable note in a consumer loan transaction. In rare instances abuses might arise in a transaction where a buyer chooses to borrow from a third person and use the loan proceeds to buy goods. Although the lender in such circumstances will probably be completely independent of the seller,[132] there is a possibility that the provision prohibiting negotiable notes in consumer sales will be evaded by subterfuge, such as use by the selling organization of a note which names the financer as payee or the referral of the buyer to a related financing organization to arrange his own financing.[133]

---

129 *See* U3C § 2.403, Comment.

130 Some clever financer might resort to use of a series of time drafts or possibly postdated checks as an attempt to circumvent the restriction.

131 The purpose of the exception relating to a sale or lease primarily for an agricultural purpose is also none too clear.

132 Where a money-loaning institution lends its money directly to the purchaser of equipment for the payment of such equipment and accepts his promissory note as evidence of the indebtedness, a failure or want of consideration in the transaction on the part of the seller of the equipment without participation or knowledge on the part of the loaning institution does not constitute a valid defense in an action to collect the note, even though the note was procured from the purchaser in the first instance by the seller and the proceeds thereof were paid by the lender directly to him. Ohio Loan & Discount Co. v. Tyarks, 173 Ohio St. 564, 184 N.E.2d 374 (1962).

133 Possibly the courts could be relied upon to maintain the "spirit" of U3C § 2.403 on the ground that the substance of the transaction will be scrutinized, and that only a completely independent lender dealing directly with the buyer may take a negotiable note as holder in due course.

D. *Waiver of Defense Where Obligation Is Transferred*

Related to the negotiable instrument problem is the question of what effect should be given to a buyer's agreement not to assert any claim or defense arising out of the sale against a transferee of the obligation.[134] Two alternatives have been proposed. The first gives limited and delayed effect to an agreement not to assert a defense. Such an agreement only becomes effective six months after the transferee has given a prescribed notice to the buyer or lessee. Prior to that time the defense may be asserted. If the transferee is "related" to the seller or lessor,[135] or a continued course of complaints in connection with other transactions by the same seller or lessor is known to the transferee, the agreement not to assert a defense will be entirely inoperative.[136] The second alternative flatly makes any transferee subject to all claims and defenses against the seller or lessor, notwithstanding agreement to the contrary.[137] Where the sale or lease is primarily for an agricultural purpose, an agreement not to assert a defense may be effective under both alternatives.[138] The result of either alternative should be a closer policing by finance companies and others who discount consumer paper to satisfy themselves of the integrity and reliability of the sellers from whom they take such paper.[139]

E. *Other Contract Requirements and Prohibitions*

Certain other contract limitations are applied to sales involving credit, leases, or loans of less than 25,000 dollars, but not to

---

134 Such an agreement not to assert a defense is valid, subject to any statute or decision which establishes a different rule for buyers or lessees of consumer goods. UNIFORM COMMERCIAL CODE § 9-206(1). For a lengthy collection of decisions see Annot., 44 A.L.R.2d 8 (1955); 36 FORDHAM L. REV. 106 (1967).

135 U3C § 1.302(12) states when a person is "related" to another person, both with respect to an individual and with respect to an organization.

136 U3C § 2.404 (alternative A). In general accord, but with much shorter periods during which a waiver of defense is ineffective are the California Motor Vehicle Sales Finance Act, CAL. CIV. CODE § 2983.5 (West Supp. 1967), (15 days), N.Y. PERS. PROP. LAW §§ 302(9), 403(3) (McKinney 1962) (10 days with respect to retail installment sales generally and sales of motor vehicles).

137 U3C § 2.404 (alternative B), the text of which is virtually identical with that of the Unruh Act of California regulating retail installment sales of goods other than motor vehicles. CAL. CIV. CODE § 1804.2 (West Supp. 1967). A similar provision exists in Oregon, ORE. REV. STATS. § 83.150 (1965). With respect to motor vehicle retail installment sales, Oregon in effect prohibits negotiable notes. ORE. REV. STATS. § 83.650 (1965).

138 U3C § 2.404 (alternatives A and B).

139 A financer may discount with or without recourse and may withhold discount proceeds in a reserve fund to cover off-sets arising from buyers' defenses.

real estate sales.[140] First, although contracts calling for "balloon" payments (any payment other than the first which is more than twice as large as the average of the other payments) are not prohibited, the debtor has the right to refinance at the time the payment is due without penalty or charge and under terms no less favorable than those of the original sale or loan. This does not apply to a schedule of payments adjusted to a buyer's seasonal income, to a credit transaction for agricultural purposes, or to a revolving credit.[141] A special provision makes a balloon provision at the end of a lease period void;[142] and a balloon payment may not be required in connection with a "regulated" loan of 1,000 dollars or less.[143]

There are also restrictions designed to prevent an overreaching seller or lessor from taking a security interest in goods other than those which are the subject of the credit sale or lease. A security interest may not be taken on real property in connection with a "regulated" loan of 1,000 dollars or less.[144] Moreover, with limited exceptions, only the property that is sold or leased may be security for the credit.[145] There are also restrictions on the taking of cross-collateral. A buyer may permit previously sold goods to be security for a subsequent sale, but only until the amount of debt arising from the original sale has been paid.[146] Where a buyer contracts more than one indebtedness to the same seller and the debts are consolidated, provision is made for release of the security interests in the goods represented in the respective debts.[147]

Credit sales, leases or loans secured by assignment of earnings,[148] the use of multiple agreements to obtain higher rates,[149]

---

[140] U3C §§ 2.401, 3.401.

[141] U3C §§ 2.405, 3.402.

[142] U3C § 2.406.

[143] U3C § 3.513, which requires such loans to be repayable in substantially equal installments over a maximum range of 25 months. This is the only maximum-term provision in the U3C.

[144] U3C § 3.511.

[145] U3C § 2.407.

[146] U3C § 2.408. For an example of the mischief that may arise where a creditor retains a security interest in previously sold goods as security for subsequent sales of other goods *see* Williams v. Walker-Thomas Furniture Co., 350 F.2d 445 (D.C. Cir. 1965).

[147] U3C § 2.409 (drafted in two alternatives).

[148] U3C §§ 2.410, 3.403. The sale of unpaid earnings is prohibited in U3C § 3.109.

[149] U3C §§ 2.042, 3.510. In other words, a seller or lender who is permitted by U3C §§ 2.201(2)(a), 3.508(2)(a) to charge a certain rate on the first $300 may not charge the same maximum rate on a $600 credit by setting up two different $300 sales or loans.

and the use of judgment notes or cognovit notes in consumer credit transactions[150] are declared void. Default charges may not by contract be made higher than the rates authorized by the U3C.[151] A provision for attorneys' fees may be set forth in a consumer credit agreement if limited to fifteen percent of the unpaid debt,[152] but no attorneys' fees may be agreed upon in connection with a "regulated" loan of 1,000 dollars or less.[153] The debtor is authorized to pay the original seller, lessor, or lender until he receives notice of the transfer of the obligation and a direction to make payment to the transferee.[154]

Two other provisions which might be said to limit traditional freedom of contract are included in the U3C. The first is directed to referral sales[155] and prohibits the giving of a rebate, discount, or other value to the buyer or lessee for the furnishing of prospects' names or otherwise aiding in the making of other sales if such rebate, discount or other value ". . . is contingent upon the occurrence of an event subsequent to the time the buyer or lessee agrees to buy or lease."[156] The other provision is an "unconscionability" section, generally applicable to an agreement or any clause thereof in connection with any consumer credit sale, consumer lease, or consumer loan, which, like the similar "unconscionability" provision of the Uniform Commercial Code,[157] permits a court to

---

150 U3C §§ 2.415, 3.407. Judgment notes are generally permitted in Ohio. 40 OHIO JUR. 2d *Negotiable Instruments* § 154 (1967).

151 U3C §§ 2.414, 3.405.

152 U3C §§ 2.413, 3.404. Reasonable expenses may also be collected.

This represents a change in Ohio law which, unlike the law of some other jurisdictions, does not give effect to provisions in notes or other obligations for the collection of attorney's fees. 40 OHIO JUR. 2d *Negotiable Instruments* § 133 (1967).

153 U3C § 3.512.

154 U3C §§ 2.412, 3.406, which give the debtor the same rights as are given the debtor in a secured transaction under UNIFORM COMMERCIAL CODE § 9-318(3), where there is an assignment of a security interest.

155 For cases dealing with this sometimes unsavory practice of making an overpriced sale coupled with a promise (often never carried out) to rebate for any referrals to other prospects by the buyer that also result in a sale see Norman v. World Wide Distrib., Inc., 202 Pa. Super. 53, 195 A.2d 115 (1963); Sherwood & Roberts Yakima, Inc. v. Leach, 67 Wash. 2d 630, 409 P.2d 160 (1965); Annot., 14 A.L.R.3d 1420 (1967).

156 U3C § 2.411.

157 UNIFORM COMMERCIAL CODE § 2.302, which was applied or at least furthered the action of the court in such "consumer credit" cases as American Home Improvement, Inc. v. MacIver, 105 N.H. 435, 201 A.2d 886 (1964); State v. ITM, Inc., 52 Misc. 2d 39, 275 N.Y.S.2d 303 (1966).

It might be noted that the Uniform Commercial Code unconscionability provision deals with the sale of goods only. There is no counterpart of Article 9 on

strike down a contract or term thereof on the ground of "unconscionability."[158] In general such limitations are desirable in that they eliminate many abuses which have made consumer-debtors the victims of overreaching or unscrupulous sellers and creditors.[159]

## VI. A Hedge Against Inflation

The U3C contains a novel and perhaps controversial provision. A number of dollar amounts stated in various sections of the Act are subject to change

> . . . in accordance with and to the extent of changes in the Consumer Price Index for Urban Wage Earners and Clerical Workers: U.S. City Average, all Items, 1957-59 = 100, compiled by the Bureau of Labor Statistics, United States Department of Labor, and hereafter referred to as the Index. The Index for December, 1967, is the Reference Base Index.[160]

The changes are to be made when there is a change in the Index of ten percent or some multiple thereof, but only changes of an even ten percent or multiple thereof are to be made. For example, a rise in the Index of ten percent could result in the raising of the maximum rate differentials to cover the first 330 dollars, rather than the first 300 dollars, at the highest rate, the amount from 330 dollars to 1,100 dollars, rather than from 300 dollars to 1,000 dollars, at the next rate, and over 1,100 dollars rather than over 1,000 dollars, at a lower maximum rate.[161]

Many, if not most, of the dollar amounts stated in various parts of the U3C are subject to similar change if the Index changes by ten percent or some multiple thereof. Substantial confusion will

---

secured transactions. *See* In re Advance Printing and Litho Company, 277 F. Supp. 101 (E.D. Pa.), *aff'd,* 387 F.2d 952 (3d Cir. 1967).

[158] U3C § 5.106. This provision is set forth as a remedial, not a substantive, section of the U3C, but it would seem to be substantive in its possible application, and might be regarded as an additional contract limitation prohibiting unconscionability.

[159] The unconscionability provision, U3C § 5.106, might be criticized, as has the similar Uniform Commercial Code provision, on the ground that it affords to a court too much discretion to make "indefinite" law. However, the Uniform Commercial Code provision has not been judicially abused to date. Moreover, several courts have indicated that a court will override an "unconscionable" contractual provision, notwithstanding the non-existence of an express statutory provision on "unconscionability." Williams v. Walker-Thomas Furniture Co., 350 F.2d 445 (D.C. Cir; 1965); Unico v. Owen, 50 N.J. 101, 232 A.2d 405 (1967), both involving pre-Uniform Commercial Code fact situations.

[160] U3C § 1.106(1).

[161] The amounts of $300 and $1,000 are declared subject to change under U3C § 1.106. *See* U3C §§ 2.201(6), 3.508(6), in all alternatives.

likely result from subjecting so many dollar amounts to change with Index variations. The benefit of providing a statutory hedge against inflation seems more than negated by such confusion. If a statutory hedge against inflation is deemed desirable, only a few of the more important dollar amounts should be so subjected. Another serious objection is that the changes will in most instances produce amounts that are not in round numbers.[162] This writer therefore suggests that the "change" provision of the U3C be either eliminated or redrafted so that changes of the Index will affect fewer dollar amounts and will be made in such a manner as to retain round figures and even-dollar amounts.

Other possible objections to the "anti-inflation" provision of the U3C deserve mention. For one thing, although it is made mandatory for the administrator or supervisor of the Uniform Consumer Credit Code in each state to issue a rule announcing the changes,[163] there is a practical problem of continuing uniformity in the U3C if it is left to the administrators of fifty states (assuming all adopt the identical text of the U3C) to declare the changes.[164] Furthermore, it might be difficult to obtain enactment of the U3C in some states if the local legislatures are to find that the sum of 300 dollars now means 330 dollars and that there is a similar change in other figures.[165] Finally, a constitutional problem might exist when the operation of a state statute is made dependent upon figures compiled by a federal bureau or agency not subject to the jurisdiction of the local legislature.[166]

## VII. Conclusion

In spite of the various criticisms which can be leveled at certain provisions of the U3C, the current draft is on the whole a

---

[162] A statutory delineation between such amounts as the first $300 and from $300 to $1,000 is handier to deal with than one between the first $330 and amounts from $330 to $1,100. Even more of a problem is a delineation that changes from small even-dollar amounts, such as $2 and $5 to amounts expressed in dollars and cents, such as $2.20 and $5.50. The latter figures represent the maximum delinquency charges which may be collected under U3C §§ 2.203(1)(a), 3.203(1)(a).

[163] U3C § 1.106(3),(4) which speaks in terms of "shall."

[164] Proceedings, *supra* note 2, at 4A-7, discussing U3C § 1.106.

[165] U3C § 1.106(4) so requires. This could also result in varying U3C § 1.106 to choose a different reference base index than that of December, 1967, if the statute is enacted in a particular state at some later time.

[166] Proceedings, *supra* note 2, at 4A. This might be deemed an unconstitutional delegation of authority to the United States Bureau of Labor Statistics, which is not charged with enforcing the U3C.

commendable and a superior job. The draftsmen have attained a workable balance between the protection of the consumer-debtor and the right of a person extending credit to have just debts repaid and to make a reasonable profit in his business of marketing money. The U3C affords consumer protections which exceed those found in most existing state statutes dealing with consumer credit;[167] yet the draftsmen and the Commissioners on Uniform State Laws take the realistic position that consumer credit should be sensibly regulated, not stifled, and that the business of extending credit to consumers is a desirable public service, notwithstanding the abuses which may occur in extension of such credit.[168]

The current draft of the Uniform Consumer Credit Code is far superior to the confused mass of diverse and piecemeal statutes which now exist;[169] and enactment of this Code in its present or similar form would represent a great stride in the development of a workable statutory pattern for control of consumer credit transactions.

---

[167] Examples are the "disclosure" provisions, the provisions dealing with home solicitation sales, those restricting such matters as judgment notes, balloon payments, referral sales, and wage assignments, as well a those prohibiting the use of negotiable notes in connection with credit sales, all discussed above.

[168] Examples include the setting of relatively high maximum rates, the furthering of competition in the consumer credit industry by such methods as "open" licensing provisions limited to lenders only, and the elimination of such traps for the unwary lender as general usury statutes, all discussed above.

[169] An analogy might be drawn by comparing Article 9 of the Uniform Commercial Code on secured transactions with the diversity of piecemeal prior statutes and rules of case law on such matters as pledges, chattel mortgages, conditional sales, bailment leases, trust receipts, assignments of accounts receivable, and factor's liens. Article 9 is not perfect and has generated considerable criticism; yet, it represents substantial improvement over former secured transactions law. In the same way, the U3C represents substantial improvement over prior consumer credit law.

# THE U3C–IT MAY LOOK PRETTY, BUT IS IT ENFORCEABLE?

John A. Spanogle, Jr.*

It is axiomatic that no regulatory legislation can be stronger than its enforcement provisions. A statute may include many excellent provisions regulating conduct, but these provisions will be meaningless if the statute does not also provide for their effective enforcement. The National Conference of Commissioners on Uniform State Laws is currently drafting a Uniform Consumer Credit Code (hereafter called the U3C)[1] to regulate the practices of those who lend to consumers. This Code is supposed to replace all present legislation regulating such lenders—small loan acts, retail installment sales acts, truth-in-lending statutes, etc. There will undoubtedly be many articles written comparing the regulatory provisions of the present statutes with those of the U3C. However, all of these comparisons of regulatory provisions are dependent not only upon the relative merits of the provisions themselves, but also upon the relative powers available for their enforcement. This article will examine the enforcement provisions available under the U3C and their effectiveness.

A regulatory statute may be enforced through many different devices. For example, different people can act against violators—either public agencies or private individuals. The enforcer may seek different types of remedies. He may seek only to prevent presently-occurring violations from recurring, or to redress the effects of past violations, or to punish past violations and therefore attempt to deter future violations; or he may seek some combination of these three powers. This article will examine the utility of these alternatives, the devices and powers needed to effectuate them,[2] and how effectively the U3C does or does not provide for them. Suggestions for change will follow.

The primary policy question presented by the U3C is whether

---

* Professor of Law, University of Maine School of Law. The author wishes to thank Mr. Robert Walker for his assistance in preparing this article.

1 UNIFORM CONSUMER CREDIT CODE (Working Draft No. 6, 1967) [hereafter cited as the U3C to distinguish it clearly from the Uniform Commercial Code, the UCC. There is no standard citation form, but a number of journals have adopted this form].

2 Thus this article will avoid discussion of the regulatory provisions of the U3C whenever possible, as being outside its scope. Two classic enforcement devices will also not be covered in detail: (1) licensing and (2) criminal penalties. *But see* notes 43, 104, and 157 *infra*. It will also avoid discussion of internal agency structure, and procedures for agency proceedings.

both public and private enforcement should be available in a consumer protection statute. The draftsmen seem to have decided that only public enforcement powers are needed, and have accordingly reduced the enforcement powers available to individual aggrieved consumers. Thus the present draft will be effective only in those states having a well-financed, aggressive, consumer-oriented Administrator. It seems unlikely that *all* Administrators in 50 states for the next 40 years will meet these criteria. Even those who do possess all the necessary attributes will find that their own powers are limited, and that the range of tools available to enforce the U3C through agency action is limited.

## I. WHAT ENFORCEMENT POWERS ARE EITHER NECESSARY OR USEFUL?

Since a regulatory statute may be enforced either publicly or privately, or both, the first question to consider is what persons should be allowed to act against violators of the statute. In addition, four functions should be performed by the enforcement provisions of a regulatory statute: (1) It must provide a method of informing the persons regulated concerning proposed courses of conduct and whether they violate the statute. (2) It must provide a method of stopping violations once they occur, and assuring that they will not reoccur. If possible, it should also provide a method of restraining violations before they occur. (3) It should provide a method of deterring violations before they occur by penalizing violators. (4) It must provide a method of redressing the effects of violations, and of compensating the aggrieved party. The second question is what statutory provisions are necessary to accomplish each function. Since the method of accomplishing these functions will be different for public and for private enforcement, the statutory provisions needed for each type of enforcement will be discussed separately.

### A. *Who Should Enforce?*

Is a public agency needed to enforce a consumer credit code? There is general agreement that the majority of consumers do not know their present rights against creditors, and even when they know of a violation are often unable or unwilling to confront the creditor.[3] In a field where the creditor is a professional, consumers are amateurs

---

3 That this is particularly true of the low-income buyer is evidenced by the finding in one study that, although forty percent of poor consumers reported exploitation in their credit purchases, over half took no retaliatory steps and only nine percent sought any form of professional help. D. CAPLOVITZ, THE POOR PAY MORE 137-140, 171 (1963).

at protecting themselves and unable to provide such protection consistently. Thus a professional is needed to protect the public interest consistently—an agency whose job it is to enforce the consumer's rights under the statute. The agency should be fully staffed with full-time personnel. It has been objected that merchants should not be subject to such regulation,[4] presumably because they too are amateurs at the lending business and do so only because of customer demand. Unfortunately, this objection ignores the present scope of installment selling,[5] the number of consumer abuses it has produced,[6] and the number of consumers adversely affected by the abuses.[7] In short, the problem has grown too large for amateur solutions randomly raised in an *ad hoc* manner.[8]

If enforcement by a public agency is provided, is private enforcement needed also? There are significant dangers in any system using only public enforcement which require that it be supplemented by provisions for effective potential private enforcement. Industry domination of its administrative agency is a well-known phenomenon.[9] Sometimes this is accomplished through the appointment of a "captive" commissioner.[10] However, more often it is accomplished through less reprehensible means. The commissioner of a consumer credit code is likely to be the banking commissioner or his sub-

---

[4] NATIONAL CONFERENCE OF COMMISSIONER ON UNIFORM STATE LAWS, PROCEEDINGS: PUBLIC HEARING ON SECOND TENTATIVE DRAFT OF THE UNIFORM CONSUMER CREDIT CODE Part 6, at 347B, 349, 353, 353A (June 16-17, 1967).

[5] Installment credit extended as of December 1967 totaled 77.946 billion dollars. This figure does not include the rapidly expanding total of credit extended by means of charge accounts. 54 FED. RES. BULL. No. 2, at A-52 (1968).

[6] *See* Art. 2 of the U3C and retail installment acts generally by means of which thirty-five states regulate automobile finance charges and twenty-six regulate other installment credit charges. Johnson, *Regulation of Finance Charges on Consumer Instalment Credit*, 66 MICH. L. REV. 81, 87 (1967).

[7] *E.g.*, the Michigan Consumer Protection Division of the Office of the Attorney General processed 1,054 complaints in 1965 while in Washington over 6,000 complaints have been incorporated into the files of the Consumer Protection Division since its creation in 1961. LEGISLATIVE COUNCIL, REPORT TO THE COLORADO GENERAL ASSEMBLY, CONSUMER PROBLEMS IN COLORADO, RESEARCH PUBLICATION No. 112 at 150, 159 (Nov. 1966).

[8] *See, e.g.*, 16 FLA. STAT. ANN. § 520.332 (Supp. 1968); IND. STAT. ANN. § 58-925 (1962); MASS. LAWS ANN. ch. 255D § 6 (1968).

[9] *See, e.g.*, Huntington, *The Marasmus of the ICC: The Commission, The Railroads, and the Public Interest*, 61 YALE L.J. 467 (1952).

[10] *See* W. CARY, POLITICS AND THE REGULATORY AGENCIES 67-68 (1967); Reich, *The New Property*, 73 YALE L.J. 733, 768 (1964); Boston Herald, Dec. 19, 1966, at 1.

ordinate, or to be selected in approximately the same manner.[11] In many states, such a commissioner must have had long experience in the credit industry, usually working for a creditor.[12] With such a background, the commissioner could have an orientation toward creditors' problems and be more "understanding" of creditor violations than the consumer.

In either case, it is unlikely that such a commissioner would be an aggressive "ombudsman" representing the consumer, thus reducing the consumer's protection to a minimal or an illusory level. The consumer needs more than enforcement of those provisions of the statute which are clear against violations which are equally clear. He also needs protection against questionable conduct by creditors, which requires test cases where the statute is unclear, or even silent, and the creditor's conduct is ambiguous. It also requires the development of new theories supporting action, and this may be accomplished only by those who view the transactions as consumers.

Even where the industry does not dominate the agency, there are necessary benefits from effective private enforcement. First, it allows the consumer to act on his own initiative, either to deter or to seek cessation of violations and redress. He does not have to obtain the prior approval or cooperation of the agency, rely upon the quality of its staff, or overcome its inertia, red tape and conservatism.[13] Secondly, it manifoldly increases the potential enforcement powers. Few agencies have sufficient funds or manpower to maintain adequate surveillance or to bring action against most violations discovered.[14] Effective private enforcement would create thousands of additional investigators and the local bar would provide many additional prosecutors. Thirdly, it is more certain to provide appropriate re-

---

11 This, at least, has been the experience under the Small Loan Acts, and there is no provision in the U3C which attempts to change the trend. ME. REV. STAT. ANN. tit. 9 §§ 222(2), 3121-22 (1964). *See also* DEL. CODE ANN. tit. 5 § 2107 (1953); N.Y. BANK. LAW § 360 (McKinney 1950).

12 ME. REV. STAT. tit. 9 § 1 (Supp. 1967). *See also* GA. CODE ANN. 13-304 (1966); IOWA CODE ANN. § 524.2 (1949).

13 This may be the meaning of the language in the Prefatory Note to *Working Draft No. 6*, U3C at 3, [hereafter cited as Prefatory Note, U3C] suggesting a necessity for ample "self-executing judicial remedies."

14 The utility, and even necessity, of this aspect of private policing is best exemplified in the area of antitrust regulation. The Antitrust Division staff would have to be quadrupled to provide enforcement solely through public agency action. Barber, *Private Enforcement of the Antitrust Laws: The Robinson-Patman Experience*, 30 GEO. WASH. L. REV. 181, 183 n.10 (1961); Wham, *Antitrust Treble Damage Suits: The Government's Chief Aid in Enforcement*, 40 A.B.A.J. 1061 (1954).

dress to the individual, especially if the agency does not have sufficient authority to seek redress easily,[15] or redress involves an election by the consumer.[16]

Further, the arguments advanced against effective private enforcement do not show any adverse effect upon legitimate creditor interests. A common argument for limiting private actions is that they have not been used sufficiently in the past to be worth the political and psychological strain of trying, over creditor opposition, to provide them. This ignores any influence consumers or consumer groups may have,[17] but, more important, it ignores the needs of the consuming public. Is past use, or lack of use, relevant if private actions can assist the agency when used? Even as to the fact of non-use, new procedures and programs, such as class actions,[18] legal aid offices and OEO neighborhood law offices, may soon render past experience irrelevant by making opportunities to seek redress more readily available.[19]

Another argument often raised for limiting private enforcement provisions is that forfeiture of both principal and interest for any violation is the usual remedy given for successful private actions, and this is too harsh a penalty.[20] However, this argument assumes that effective private enforcement requires such a remedy in all circumstances—an unwarranted assumption, as will be shown below.[21] Instead, it is quite possible to provide a set of graduated sanctions to the consumer, to provide different deterrent effects in different circumstances.

---

15 *See* text at notes 92-97 *infra.*

16 *See* text following note 144 *infra.*

17 NAT'L LEGAL AID AND DEFENDER ASS'N, JOINT STATEMENT OF NLDA AND OEO LEGAL SERVICES PROGRAM RE WORKING DRAFT NO. 6 OF UCCC (January 10, 1968).

18 That the class action device is intended for and adapted to the protection of small claimants is discussed in Dolgow v. Anderson, 43 F.R.D. 472, 494-95 (E.D.N.Y. 1968) (a class action on behalf of allegedly defrauded securities purchasers authorized by FED. R. CIV. P. 23).

19 The conclusion that there has in fact been a lack of use in the past is also open to question. It is primarily based on the absence of reported appellate cases, but this does not indicate its utility at the trial court level, especially in small claims courts. Further, it ignores any non-judicial use of such opportunities to influence out-of-court settlements. Finally, it cannot measure the *in terrorem* influence of potential actions to inhibit violations. Thus the case of past non-use is at best unproved.

20 Most Small Loan Acts so provided. F. HUBACHEK, ANNOTATIONS ON SMALL LOAN LAWS (Based on Sixth Draft of the Uniform Small Loan Law) 119-25 (1938). It is believed that this inhibited public enforcement.

21 See text at notes 52-59, *infra.*

Thus a combination of both public and private enforcement powers should be provided so that each can supplement the other. Each can perform different functions, and each must be examined separately to determine its capability of informing creditors and halting, deterring and redressing violations of the statute.

## B. *Public Enforcement Provisions*

As to the informational function, the vast bulk of creditors will adhere to any regulations if they both know and understand their effect.[22] Thus, the first requisite to any workable enforcement scheme is to provide this information to creditors, and only a public agency can furnish a consistent interpretation. The information can be either general, relating to classes of problems, or specific, providing answers to individual inquiries concerning particular proposed courses of conduct. The agency must be able to provide both. General regulations, however detailed, cannot answer specific questions, because the methods óf merchandising and lending to the consumer are too diverse to fit any set of standard patterns. The agency must therefore be empowered to issue advice in response to queries, and also to issue formal declaratory orders. The creditors should be furnished a clear procedure for raising such questions.[23]

Information must be available both on an informal and on a formal basis, so that the creditor can obtain not only advice but also a declaratory order. A declaratory order may be appealed from, but advice or an advisory opinion typically may not.[24] Without declaratory orders which are appealable under the applicable statute, there is no method of testing the agency beliefs in courts without first violating the statute. If the informational function is to be properly served, it should be available before the creditor violates the statute, especially if other methods can be easily provided. In the consumer field this may be especially important, because many merchants and other creditors are conscious of consumer good will and would prefer not to risk it by deliberately violating a statute if such conduct can be avoided. A second, and less important, reason for declaratory

---

[22] Felsenfeld, *Some Ruminations About Remedies in Consumer-Credit Transactions*, 8 B.C. IND. & COM. L. REV. 535 (1967).

[23] Although many states have administrative procedure acts which would provide procedures for declaratory orders, a uniform act must provide such procedures for states which do not have them. *See* W. GELLHORN & C. BYSE, ADMINISTRATIVE LAW, app. II, at 1231 (1960).

[24] 1 K. DAVIS, ADMINISTRATIVE LAW TREATISE §§ 4.09, 4.10 (1958) [hereinafter cited as DAVIS].

orders is that, if they are favorable, the creditor should be able to rely on them and be protected from agency action against conduct based on them. The orders should be subject to rescission after notice and hearing, to provide flexibility in a field of rapidly changing social values, but they should protect from agency action as long as they are effective. The declaratory orders cannot preclude consumer test cases in court, and may be invalidated by the courts.[25]

It would probably be unwise, however, to require the agency to issue such orders in all cases. Where the facts are predeterminable and not easily modified, such as proposed creditor's forms or interest rate structures, there seems no problem in requiring an order. On the other hand, where the facts are fluid, such as proposed sales techniques or debt collection tactics, the agency probably should not give an unqualified assurance, since statutory compliance can only be judged on the basis of actual conduct. Thus declaratory orders should be mandatory only for a limited class of inquiries.[26]

If a creditor violates the statute or threatens to do so, the agency's first concern should be to prevent the violations, or halt them and prevent their recurrence. A wide range of devices must be provided the agency because it will face a wide variety of situations involving violations. Some will involve misinterpretations of the statute; others deliberate abuses of consumers. Both informal and formal procedures will be needed, involving both internal agency proceedings and direct access to the courts, and permitting effective voluntary settlements as well as enforcement through litigation. Above all, in the many circumstances where mass public harm is threatened, for example false advertising, the agency must be able to act very quickly to protect the public interest effectively.

One informal method of halting violations is to accept an assurance of discontinuance from the creditor. In effect, the agency accepts the creditor's promise to behave as a substitute for an order

25 Neither the principles of *res judicata* nor those of collateral estoppel would apply to bar the consumer's private suit since he was not a party nor privy to the original declaratory proceeding. *See,* RESTATEMENT OF JUDGMENTS § 93 and comments at 460-67 (1942). As to the *res judicata* effect of a declaratory proceeding between the Administrator and a party to the order see L. JAFFE & N. NATHANSON, ADMINISTRATIVE LAW: CASES AND MATERIALS 410 (2d ed. 1961).

26 REVISED MODEL STATE ADMINISTRATIVE PROCEDURE ACT § 8 (1961). If mandatory for a limited class, the class could be determined by designating those sections of the U3C which relate to the form of contracts, and omitting those sections which relate to other creditor conduct. *But cf.,* Note, *The Availability and Reviewability of Rulings of the Internal Revenue Service,* 113 U. PA. L. REV. 81 (1964).

resulting from more formal proceedings, but without the expense of those formal proceedings. Since this device will be accepted in a negotiating context, rather than in litigation, the agency must be able to resolve fairly all issues relating to injuries to the public interest while it is negotiating and deciding whether to accept the assurance. Thus it should be able to condition its acceptance upon obtaining admissions of the prior violations,[27] redress to all consumers aggrieved by prior violations,[28] and reimbursement to the agency for money spent investigating the prior violations.[29] In addition, some consideration should be given to the losses which can be caused by future violations. Thus, in appropriate situations, another possible condition should be the establishment of an escrow fund to provide redress and cover investigation expenses of proven future violations.[30]

A more formal method of halting violations is the cease and desist order, issued after notice and a hearing. Use of an agency proceeding, rather than a court proceeding, allows fact-finding by a tribunal which specializes in such problems, and may therefore be more aware of the business setting of the problem and the ramifications of its rulings.[31] The agency must be able to act on its own initiative, without a complaint from an aggrieved consumer.[32] The orders need not be self-executing and will in any event be subject to judicial review.[33] The review of findings of fact should be on the record made in the agency, and the agency's expertise should be

---

27 The use of an admission as a *prima facie* case in subsequent proceedings is granted to the New York attorney general in his public enforcement role. N.Y. Exec. Law § 63(15) (McKinney Supp. 1967).

28 The State's interest in private redress is a function of its concern with public welfare, a recognized area for exercise of the police power. Mass. Laws Ann. ch. 93A § 5 (Supp. 1967); Vt. Stat. Ann. tit. 9 § 2459 (Supp. 1968).

29 Authorities cited *supra* note 28. The New York attorney general may make the payment of such costs a condition to his acceptance of an assurance of discontinuance in lieu of prosecution for a violation of state law. N.Y. Exec. Law § 63(15) (McKinney Supp. 1967).

30 Such a procedure was suggested and adopted for use by the New York Consumer Frauds Bureau. Memorandum of N.Y. Dept. of Law, 1965 McKinney's Session Laws of New York 2070; N.Y. State Finance Law § 121(2)o (McKinney Supp. 1966). Such a provision should not be considered a penalty, since the UCC provides that an analogous "guaranty" may be required as part of an assurance of performance in a commercial transaction. Uniform Commercial Code § 2-609, Comment 4.

31 1 Davis, *supra* note 24, § 1.05 at 37-40.

32 Not all Administrators are authorized to act on their own initiative. *See, e.g.,* Md. Code Ann. art. 83 § 162(a) and (d) (1965).

33 3 Davis, *supra* note 24, § 29.11.

recognized by adoption of the customary rule of upholding the agency action if supported by credible evidence in the record.[34]

If the cease and desist orders are not self-executing, it will be necessary to seek a court order for enforcement. This would require two hearings and two notice periods before the violation is halted. In many situations, such a lengthy reaction time will be unsatisfactory; something quicker is needed to protect the public from future mass violations. Thus the agency should be able to approach a court directly, and on its own initiative, to seek to halt violations. It should be able to seek temporary relief pending a hearing, under the normal limitations traditionally provided by an equity court.[35] As an additional violation-prevention device, the agency should be able to seize and condemn any forms or advertising matter not in compliance with the statute.[36] All such relief should be available to the agency on its own initiative, without any prior complaints from aggrieved consumers, because the purpose of agency enforcement is to obviate the necessity of reliance on consumer initiatives. Thus it should be able to provide continuous and consistent surveillance and enforcement, regardless of the ability or willingness of the consuming public to protect itself.

A second problem concerns the scope of the order. An order merely to discontinue the exact form of present violation will often be illusory, because a creditor may then change his practices slightly and escape any effect of the order while still violating the statute. Thus, the agency should be able to issue orders which cover practices similar to the illegal acts which have actually occurred.[37]

In addition to halting the violations, the agency should be able to redress past violations. This requires that it have power to strike

---

34 *Id.*

35 *See, e.g.,* FED. R. CIV. P. 65(b); authorities cited *infra* note 89. One example of the required "immediate and irreparable injury" is a mass fraudulent advertising campaign.

36 *See, e.g.,* the Federal provisions for seizure and forfeiture of "containers, vehicles and vessels" involved in violations of liquor transportation laws. 18 U.S.C. § 3615 (1964).

37 The cease and desist orders of some Federal agencies have been challenged on the ground of overbreadth, but despite the fact that violation of the order would subject the party to the summary penalty of a contempt decree broad language has been upheld. For a general discussion of this issue see FTC v. Colgate-Palmolive Co., 380 U.S. 374, 392-95 (1965). On the State level a similarly broadly worded injunction, which traditionally must be specific, was upheld prohibiting demanding, receiving or attempting to collect usurious interest, or charging or contracting for any usurious interest. Wilson Finance Co. v. State, 342 S.W.2d 117 (Tex. Civ. App. 1960).

prohibited clauses from contracts already in existence or seek injunctions against their enforcement, to require refunds of overcharges, and to obtain rescission or cancellation of prohibited types of contracts in appropriate cases. Where appropriate redress requires an election by the consumer, such as to rescind a contract or not,[38] the agency must also be able to contact the consumer and obtain his decision. Its ability to provide such redress can relieve the consumer of the burden of initiating action to seek relief from either the creditor or the courts, thereby raising the probability that the individual consumer's rights will be protected. The agency should also be able to obtain redress for itself.[39] The investigation and prosecution of the creditor has required expenditures, and it should be reimbursed if the creditor has violated the statute. Such expenses should be borne by the creditor who caused them, rather than the public at large. Reimbursement increases the agency's resources and discourages any attempt to defeat enforcement through exhaustion of the agency's resources, as through numerous appeals.

Where the agency seeks both to halt violations and to redress past violations, this should not require separate actions. Thus, at the informal level of enforcement, acceptance of an assurance of discontinuance could be conditioned on providing redress to all individual aggrieved consumers. In agency proceedings, the agency should be able to issue an order for redress as well as a cease and desist order. In court, if the agency can represent the aggrieved consumers as a class, it can obtain redress for them while obtaining an injunction against creditor conduct. If separate actions are required in any of these cases, the extra drain on agency resources will limit the number of cases it can attempt to resolve.

Providing the agency with a deterrent capability is also a necessity because simply stopping the present violations or preventing their recurrence, or even providing redress for past violations, is sometimes inappropriate. Lack of a deterrent allows the creditor to violate the statute literally without risk. If he is later ordered to stop, or even ordered to redress violations, he has lost nothing more than his ill-gotten gains. Where he has nothing to lose by violating the statute, he is less likely to be careful in observing the consumer's rights. Any system which depends upon stopping a course of prohibited conduct after it occurs is not effective at halting the first violations. Agency inertia or lack of manpower may allow these prior

---

38 See text following note 144 *infra*.

39 MD. CODE ANN. art. 83 § 25 (Supp. 1967).

violations to continue for an extended time. Thus, the agency must be given the ability to penalize past violations, thereby deterring future violations.

Once the creditor has an opportunity to seek a declaratory order on the propriety of any particular course of dealing, liability should attach to any conduct which violates the statute. It may be objected that most creditors are honest and should not be penalized for honest mistakes, and that penalties should not be available unless some form of *mens rea* can be proved.[40] Such a limitation is not relevant where declaratory orders are available. The limitation is based on a belief that it is unjust to penalize for the first violation, because the violator could not be certain that his conduct was illegal until a court had so ruled. However, if declaratory orders are provided, the creditor has a method of obtaining a ruling on the validity of his proposed conduct before acting. If he chooses either not to seek such a ruling or to ignore a ruling before engaging in conduct so questionable that it is later found illegal, a sanction should be available.[41] The purpose of a regulatory statute is to inhibit creditors from carelessly engaging in questionable conduct, so that lack of prior agency approval should be the only condition to liability for some penalty. With regard to public enforcement, the agency is unlikely to penalize a single clerical error arising under circumstances unlikely to recur, as long as it is given discretion in such matters. Thus, the agency should be able to seek sanctions against all violating conduct not protected by a ruling, regardless of "willfulness" but at its discretion.[42]

What sanctions should be available? Obviously, the penalty should be designed to fit the type of violation. But there are an almost infinite number of relevant independent variables—the seriousness of the type of violation, the number of occurrences, the prior history of violations by the same creditor, the deliberateness of his conduct, his willingness to halt violations and offer redress to consumers, the necessity of litigation, and others. It must be recognized that the like-

---

40 *Cf.* U3C § 6.113(3), (4).

41 A different analysis may apply when the creditor has sought a declaratory order, but has been unable to obtain one because the agency feels it cannot give a sufficiently concrete and unqualified opinion to serve any purpose. See note 25 *supra.* In this limited class of circumstances, imposing a penalty without a *mens rea* requirement would depend solely upon whether the legislature desired to use absolute liability concepts in this area. See text at note 64 *infra.*

42 Such discretion would obviate the problems encountered under most Small Loan Acts. See note 20 *supra.*

lihood of discovery of violations is relevant, and will vary from state to state. No agency can afford to undertake complete surveillance or to litigate all violations discovered. In states where investigations and enforcement are more extensive, an effective deterrent can be provided by use of smaller sanctions than in states where money and manpower, and therefore the chances of discovery and enforcement, are limited. Thus the extent of the penalty given through public enforcement cannot be set by statute but must be discretionary. The maximum penalties should be sufficiently great to deter prohibited conduct,[43] but the agency should be allowed to seek lesser penalties where it sees fit.

## C. *Private Enforcement Provisions*

The powers necessary to create effective private enforcement are different and must be analyzed differently. One difference is that the consumer cannot perform the informational function. Moreover, he cannot be bound by the agency's declaratory orders, because he had no opportunity to be heard before their issuance.[44] If private enforcement is the antidote to possible industry domination or agency inertia, red tape or conservatism, the declaratory order cannot bar private actions.[45] Further, if private actions are to serve an effective

---

43 The possible sanctions include: (1) a civil penalty, (2) a criminal penalty and (3) revocation of a license. Each presents problems concerning effective use. The civil penalty, if imposed, may easily be written off as just another cost of doing business, especially if the maximum is low and the chance of enforcement small. This device is effective only if a penalty may be levied for each individual violation. As a minimum, in all cases, the Administrator should be able to recover all the costs of investigating and prosecuting the violating creditor. Although this merely provides redress for the Administrator, it is a penalty to the creditor.

Criminal sanctions and revocation of license cannot be dismissed in the same way. They are, however, often dismissed on the ground that they are little used in practice. Felsenfeld, *supra* note 22. Such reactions may not, however, portray the complete picture. For example, an attorney's advice to a client regarding a proposed course of questionable conduct may be far less cautious when only money is being risked than if criminal sanctions, and the attendant publicity, could be involved, even though a criminal action has never been brought in the state.

44 See note 25 *supra.*

45 Declaratory orders are generally treated as the same as other agency adjudications, *e.g.*, Federal Administrative Procedure Act, 5 U.S.C. § 554(e) (1966). It does not necessarily follow, however, that it is the product of a genuine adversary proceeding. And while the agency is bound to protect the interests of consumers generally, it cannot be presumed to have asserted and protected the interests of any particular consumer. Compare the problem of inadequate representation in spurious class actions, FED. R. CIV. P. 23(a).

purpose, the declaratory order cannot defeat those parts of the individual's recovery which seek to compensate him for the expenses of such action or induce him to undertake the risks thereof.[46]

Once violations occur or are threatened, however, consumers have an interest in halting or preventing them to at least the same extent as the regulatory agency. The typical device available to groups of individuals to prevent harm to the group is the class action, but this is not available for prospective enforcement in its normal state.[47] Some of the problems are technical and relate only to use of the normal class action device as such,[48] and can be obviated by expressly granting a right to enjoin the violation to an aggrieved consumer.[49] Would a grant of such a right be wise? It would permit consumers to halt violations, and would also allow them to show the entire pattern of operations of a violating creditor, which might be necessary to overcome limitations on obtaining redress or imposing sanctions under the statute.[50] On the other hand, prospective enforcement through private ombudsmen is not generally permitted. If "all the world" are potential victims, assuring adequate representation is difficult. Preclusion of subsequent actions by those claiming non-representation is also difficult, and could provide opportunity for collusion. If multiple injunction actions are allowed, the burden on the creditor and the opportunity for harassment of the non-violating creditor are also great. However, limiting the right of action to consumers already aggrieved by the violations and requiring the posting of a bond to cover a successful creditor's costs could greatly reduce such problems.[51]

The consumer's primary interest is in obtaining redress for the

---

[46] See text at notes 52-60 *infra.*

[47] The primary problem is one of standing. See discussion in text at note 110 *infra.*

[48] *E.g.,* in addition to the standing problem, can anyone assure adequate representation of an unborn potential victim, within FED. R. CIV. P. 23?

[49] *See* N. MEX. STAT. 49-15-8 (Supp. 1968) which allows an individual to enjoin "deceptive trade practices" of another if he is "likely" to be damaged thereby. *See also* Dole, *Merchant and Consumer Protection: The Uniform Deceptive Trade Practices Act,* 76 YALE L.J. 485, 495-501 (1967).

[50] Although such limitations ought not to be placed on the consumer's right to recover, see text at notes 63, 64 *infra,* the present draft of the U3C does so limit them. U3C § 5.201.

[51] For a far deeper and more illuminating discussion of these problems than is practicable for this article, generally affirming the consumer's right to enjoin, if properly limited, see Starrs, *The Consumer Class Action: Considerations of Equity and Procedure,* NAT'L INST. OF EDUC. IN LAW AND POVERTY, HANDBOOK ON CONSUMER LAW § 74.2, at 23 (1968).

violations of his rights. But this involves more than refunding an overcharge or striking a prohibited clause from a contract. The consumer whose statutory rights have been violated must be not only made aware of the violation, but also willing and able to confront the creditor and seek redress. Even after deciding to seek redress, he can still lose all if he does not choose a response permitted by the statute. If not aided by counsel, the violation might never be discovered or the creditor confronted; and even if he seeks redress, the unadvised consumer's instinctive reaction is to stop paying the debt, which creates a default and all the creditor's remedies which arise therefrom. Thus, any consumer protection statute must recognize the necessity for the aggrieved consumer to consult an attorney, even in the case which is settled out of court, and must actively seek to promote such conduct.[52]

Attorneys, however, charge fees, and the fee for redressing the creditor's violation will come out of the aggrieved consumer's pocket. Thus, the consumer must invest money to obtain a redress of the violation, even when litigation is not involved. He must also invest time and risk his reputation and good will with the local credit industry. If he receives only a refund of an overcharge or the striking of a void clause from his contract, he has not been made whole. He has still lost the amount of his attorney's fee, his time, reputation and good will. Something more is needed even in the settlement situation, if the statute is to promote solution of these problems through legal channels.[53] This "something more" should compensate him for both attorney's fees and time and risk to reputation. Three methods of providing such an additional award seem possible: (1) an additional award related to attorney's fees, either "a reasonable attorney's fee" or a stated dollar amount related to a typical fee for handling such a problem; (2) cancellation of the interest charge; (3) an option for the consumer to rescind the contract.[54]

---

52 Of course, some consumers are sufficiently sophisticated to recognize violations and confront the creditor to seek adjustment. This adjustment may then be negotiated without regard to the remedy provisions of any statute and to the mutual satisfaction of the parties. Where they can deal on equal terms, this resolution may be more appropriate than any statutory rule; but it is an atypical fact situation.

53 This is not the same measure of damages which would be given by the standard contract formulation. However, damages established by a statute's regulatory scheme can be different, and the U3C draftsmen have already recognized the necessity of differing from the standard formulation by providing recovery of attorney's fees in some circumstances. U3C § 5.201(7).

54 The term "rescind," rather than the UCC term "cancel" is used deliberately as reflecting more accurately the relief envisaged. Rescission would include return of both goods and payments, with or without an allowance for use. Since the consumer

The first method is causally related to part of the necessary compensation, but compensates him only for the monetary part of his investment. Setting a standard fee will be difficult, since the typical fee will be different in urban and rural locations. If a standard is not set, the creditor and consumer's attorney may not be able to agree on a "reasonable" fee without the mediating influence of a court. Out-of-court settlements can be promoted only if the recovery amounts are explicit and very certain. The second method is not causally related to any part of the consumer's investment, but might compensate him for all facets of his investment in many cases, and also is certain and easily ascertainable. However, any award relating to cancellation of an interest charge must provide for a minimum recovery. Without such a minimum, it is too easy for the seller to raise his supposed cash price and eliminate interest charges, thus avoiding the statutory penalty.[55] If the minimum is set sufficiently high to cover a typical attorney's fee, this would seem to combine the best attributes of the first two methods.

In some circumstances, however, enforcement of the contract, even with an allowance, is completely inappropriate. Where the violation relates to inducing the consumer to contract, such as a false statement of a contract term or a prohibited referral sale, there is no relationship between the consumer's loss of expectations and any monetary award. In many instances it can be presumed that the consumer would not have purchased but for the violation, so that a far more appropriate remedy would be an option to rescind.[56] Even where a monetary award could be appropriate, many aggrieved consumers will not consult an attorney, but will stop making payments— an inartistic attempted rescission. If the consumer thereby loses all protection, the statute has not aided him, regardless of the quality of its regulatory provisions. Thus it is at least arguable that such conduct should be recognized, and optional rescission allowed for all violations.[57]

---

has had to invest time and money to obtain redress, such an allowance seems inappropriate. A separate problem is created by destruction or damage of the goods sold, which could prohibit appropriate use of the rescission device.

[55] The federal Truth in Lending Act provides an example of how this may be done. 82 Stat. 146, § 130(a)(1), 1968 *United States Code, Cong. and Admin. News* 1232, 1245.

[56] See note 54 *supra*.

[57] A possible limit on such recognition arises from the fact that some technical violations, such as a small overcharge, probably will not be discovered by the consumer without aid of counsel. Rescission in such cases might therefore be inappropriate.

If the foregoing remedies are necessary to compensate the consumer fully in the out-of-court settlement situation, they are obviously insufficient when litigation is required. The investments of time and money are greater, but more important a new element is added—risk. To the layman the risks of litigation are frighteningly uncertain and create an immense psychological barrier. He must invest his time and money knowing that his chances of success are low[58] and that he cannot estimate them with any accuracy. He must be prepared to fight appeals and contend with the best legal counsel. Mere compensation for expenditures, such as an award of attorney's fees, cannot therefore realistically compensate, because it ignores the risk factor. Instead an incentive is needed to induce the consumer to undertake the risks involved, and an incentive great enough to induce him to undertake test cases to clarify the statute.[59] Such awards to the successful litigant must be very substantial to create this kind of incentive, and also to compensate him for both the large expenses and the risks he must undertake.[60]

Such additional awards will also act as a deterrent. Consumers, as a group, need such a deterrent capability more than a public agency, because they have no means of consistently halting or redressing violations. Thus, if they are to supplement the powers of an under-financed, or perhaps industry dominated, agency, they must have the power to deter violations. Providing such a deterrent capability does not necessitate a harsh penalty, such as voiding both principal and interest, in all cases. Sanctions can be differentiated depending upon the conduct one seeks to induce or deter.

In particular, the consumer has two identifiable interests which must be separately recognized. First, he has an interest in inducing the creditor not to violate the statute. Secondly, after violation, he has an interest in inducing the creditor to settle, rather than litigate. Thus, two different levels of deterrents are needed, just as two levels of redress awards are needed—one applicable to out-of-court settlements, the other to instances in which a violating creditor has compelled the consumer to litigate. Even if large deterrents are available

---

58 In the area of private antitrust litigation, for example, less than 17 per cent of plaintiffs are successful. *See* Alioto, *The Economics of A Treble Damage Case*, 32 A.B.A. ANTITRUST L.J. 87, 92 (1966).

59 Such test cases will be highly speculative, but necessary if private enforcement is to supplement the administrative agency. The agency may be conservative or jealous of its litigation record and therefore unwilling to attempt test cases.

60 In antitrust regulation, the successful litigant can obtain treble damages. 15 U.S.C. § 15 (1964). The analogy does not seem apposite in the area of consumer protection, however, because of the lack of provable commercial damages.

in the litigation context, if they are only available then, there is no deterrent applicable to the act of violating the statute. The violating creditor could settle the few claims raised by consumers without liability, which in effect permits violation without risk.[61] This ignores one purpose of such sanctions, and fails to protect an identifiable consumer interest.

On the other hand, failure to differentiate between the awards available with and without litigation will induce the creditor to threaten to litigate all complaints. Threats of such conduct, including endless appeals, will intimidate many consumers to abandon their efforts to achieve redress. Thus, serious efforts at settlement will be implemented by differentiating awards according to the method of resolution.[62] The difference between the settlement award and the litigation award is an inducement not to litigate, or a deterrent to litigation. If a court finds that the creditor has violated the statute, it must be presumed that the creditor had the power to propose an out-of-court settlement which offered full redress, as long as the aggrieved consumer made an attempt to contact the creditor and settle the grievance before initiating action. Therefore, the only condition to recovery of the larger award, other than successfully proving the violation, should be a demand by the consumer for redress and lapse of sufficient reaction time without an offer of full settlement by the creditor.

It is often proposed that such awards be conditioned on proof of "willful" violations by the creditor,[63] but the suggestion fails to perceive the multiple purposes of the awards. For example, large awards to the successful private litigant are given both to induce him to undertake the risks and expenses involved and to deter the violating creditor from requiring him to litigate. The willfulness of the original violation is therefore irrelevant to granting the award. Where the creditor settles out of court, it is arguable that willfulness should be relevant, to penalize only the culpable violator. But it is also arguable that violations of a consumer protection statute should provide absolute liability to induce the creditor to establish and maintain such business practices as may be necessary to prevent inadvertent violations, especially where the penalty is mild.[64] However, if the amount of the award is set to compensate the aggrieved con-

---

61 *See* text between notes 39 and 40 *supra.*
62 On this point, the U3C draftsmen agree *in theory.* See Comment to § 5.201.
63 *See* U3C § 5.201(6).
64 R. PERKINS, CRIMINAL LAW 692-710 (1957).

sumer for his investment of time, money and reputation in seeking redress, the award also serves a redress purpose, and willfulness is again irrelevant to granting an award for such a purpose.

Thus, a dual system of enforcement is proposed. Public enforcement is likely to provide more consistent application of control, but may not be aggressive, for it may be underfinanced or subject to bureaucratic conservatism, red tape and inertia or to industry domination. It therefore should be supplemented by effective private enforcement which, although applying only randomly, is not subject to bureaucratic control or lethargy. The public agency should first be provided a means of informing the creditor as to the validity of specific courses of proposed conduct, then provided ample means of preventing or halting violations and redressing and penalizing those which have occurred. It should have the power to handle each of these functions informally or formally through agency proceedings or in court. Several functions should be accomplished in one proceeding —for example, allowing the agency to condition its acceptance of an assurance of discontinuance on redress to aggrieved individuals, seizure of forms with prohibited clauses and establishment of an escrow fund to redress future violations.

Private individuals should be empowered to bring class actions to halt violations, within some limitations, and also to seek full redress. Any award which grants full redress must include compensation for the consumer's investment of time, money and reputation, even in achieving an out-of-court settlement, and such an award would also act as a mild deterrent. If a larger additional deterrent is desired in more specialized circumstances, it should be provided. Thus, if a violating creditor refuses to settle, a very substantial award is needed to induce the consumer to risk litigation. However, the addition of such larger awards in special circumstances should not create conditions on the recovery of the basic redress-oriented award.

## II. THE STATUTE

The enforcement provisions of the U3C are divided between two articles, Article 6 on public enforcement and Article 5 on private enforcement. Each will be discussed in turn. A stated basic assumption of the U3C draftsmen is that the statute should provide "ample administrative powers and self-executing judicial remedies" to assure compliance with the statute.[65] The intended meaning of the reference to administrative powers is clear, and the draftsmen have

---

[65] Prefatory Note, U3C at 3.

concentrated on this aspect of enforcement. However, the intended meaning of the reference to "self-executing judicial remedies" is less clear. It seems to refer to remedies available to the consumer without agency intervention, but does it refer only to remedies available without resort to courts? If the latter is intended, it is an illusory exercise, because judicial recognition of the individual's rights will usually be needed to protect them fully.

## A.  *Public Enforcement Under the U3C*

The U3C grants broad powers to an "Administrator," but does not seem to grant him the power to issue declaratory orders. He may promulgate substantive rules "in cases specifically authorized by this Act,"[66] but these are intended to be only general regulations, not responses to specific inquiries. He may also "counsel persons and groups on their rights and duties under this Act,"[67] but such counsel does not seem appealable if adverse, so the creditor must violate the advice to test it. If favorable, the informal "counsel" cannot be relied upon because it provides no protection from subsequent action by the Administrator. Thus, there is no method provided under the U3C to inform creditors whether a proposed course of specific conduct violates the statute.

General regulations may be issued, and do provide protection for all conduct conforming to a then-existing rule or guideline.[68] Such regulations may be amended, rescinded or invalidated by the Administrator or a court,[69] so that the creditor has no vested right in retaining a regulation once he has set his business practices,[70] but a subsequent change has no effect on prior creditor conduct. While the rule or guideline is in force, the creditor is protected from all liability for conforming conduct. Although this seems sound for liability through public enforcement, it improperly limits actions by individual consumers and subverts private enforcement. The "no liability" rule precludes any award to the successful consumer litigant, even to reimburse him for attorney's fees actually expended, and thereby destroys all incentive to bring private actions against

---

[66] U3C § 6.104(1)(f). Such power is specifically provided in only three instances: adjustment of dollar amounts, additional charges, and advertising. U3C §§ 1.106, 2.202, 2.303.

[67] U3C § 6.104(1)(b).

[68] U3C § 6.104(2).

[69] U3C §§ 6.104(1)(f), 6.108(2).

[70] There seems to be no requirement of notice before change of regulations so the creditor does not even have this interest.

creditors to test agency regulations.[71] Nor does the U3C provide any method for consumers to test such regulations before the agency itself. Thus, if industry domination exists, the "no liability" rule will help sustain it.

Instead of providing such information to creditors, the U3C draftsmen have concentrated on halting prohibited conduct only after a course of dealing which violates the statute has started, and then preventing such conduct from recurring. Article 6 provides for informal handling through assurances of discontinuance, for agency proceedings leading to a judicially reviewable cease and desist order, and for direct application to the courts for injunctions. Thus the necessary types of enforcement devices have been provided, but there are problems in the scope and structure of the devices set forth in the U3C.

The Administrator is allowed to deal with violators informally and accept an assurance of discontinuance from them.[72] This might have provided the Administrator a very useful enforcement tool, except that it seems to be usable only in very limited situations. The present draft allows its use only to process "conduct subject to an order by the Administrator (Section 6.108) or a court (Sections 6.110 through 6.112)."[73] This language might be interpreted to include all violations against which either might act; however, since the language is not conditional, it literally seems applicable only to those prior violations which have been the subject of actual orders directed to the particular creditor. If the latter interpretation prevails, assurances may not be used to handle claimed violations of the statute, but only claimed violations of an Administrator's order or a court order. Thus it may not be used to process the initial violations of the statute by a particular creditor, where an informal procedure would be the most useful tool to inform him of the violation and impose a mild sanction. Instead, it could only be used to process later violations, occurring after a formal proceeding, and when the creditor should be aware of the questionable nature of his conduct. This limitation requires the Administrator to handle all first violations through formal proceedings—a needless escalation of the conflict in many cases—or take no official action.

---

[71] The analytical problems presented seem quite similar to those concerning the requirement of "willfulness" for a supposedly-deterrent penalty award, which is also needed to afford complete redress to the consumer.

[72] U3C § 6.109.

[73] *Id.*

If an assurance is given and the creditor continues his violations, the prior assurance "is evidence" that violations occurred before the assurance.[74] This seems to be the only effect under the U3C of breaching an assurance. There is no express authority to condition acceptance on redress to aggrieved consumers, reimbursement to the agency for investigation costs or establishment of an escrow fund to redress future violations.[75] Since the assurance evidences prior violations, it probably cannot be worded to cover more than those violations which the Administrator is willing to attempt to prove have actually occurred in the past.[76] Thus the violator can change his prohibited practices slightly and escape the scope of the assurance. In order to use the assurance as "evidence" of prior violations, the Administrator seemingly must first prove that the assurance itself has been breached, which requires that he first prove the occurrence of the subsequent violations. Of what value, then, is the assurance? The multiple conditions on its use in court make the U3C's assurance of discontinuance an illusory regulatory tool.

Formal agency proceedings are also available, on the Administrator's initiative,[77] except against unconscionable contracts or collection tactics.[78] The reason for this exclusion is obscure, for the agency expertise would seem most useful in defining or analyzing these abstract concepts.[79] For other violations, the Administrator may, after a hearing, issue a cease and desist order, which is subject to judicial review upon appeal by the creditor.[80] The Administrator's orders are not self-executing, so he must seek a court order for enforcement. His findings of fact may be reversed only if clearly erroneous, and creditors' objections not urged at the administrative hearing are deemed waived unless excused for good cause.[81] If the

---

74 *Id.*, second sentence.

75 *See* text at notes 27-30 *supra.*

76 Compare the problems created by the scope of a cease and desist order. *See* note 37 *supra.* The problem is even more easily solved in the assurance of discontinuance context, because the admissions may be stated separately from the assurance. *See* text at note 27 *supra.* By providing for admissions, some of the problems discussed in text following this footnote may be obviated.

77 U3C § 6.108.

78 U3C § 6.108(6). *See* note 91 *infra.*

79 If it is felt that the defining of "unconscionability" should be controlled by the courts, all agency decisions are reviewable. U3C § 6.108(1). Thus the exclusion can be supported only by asserting that the courts must have the *exclusive* opportunity to develop a definition. However, such an assertion ignores the primary rationale for providing expert administrative bodies.

80 U3C § 6.108(1).

81 U3C § 6.108(2), (3).

creditor does not appeal within thirty days, the Administrator may procure a court order for enforcement by petitioning the court and showing service of the agency order on the creditor and that he is subject to the jurisdiction of the court.[82] The statute does not state whether the court must issue such an enforcement order, nor whether defenses may be interposed at this point by the creditor. At least, however, the agency order is now "final," and the Administrator need not "support its findings with substantial evidence."[83]

The primary problem created by these agency hearings is the scope of the orders provided. The cease and desist order concerns only the halting of presently-occurring violations.[84] It cannot redress aggrieved individuals, reimburse the agency, or prevent future or penalize past violations. The same is also true for the resulting court enforcement orders, for according to the statute the court may grant only a restraining order through the Administrator's petition.[85]

The Administrator also has direct access to the courts, on his own initiative, to seek a temporary or permanent injunction (but not a temporary restraining order) to halt violations of the Act.[86] Temporary relief is available only after notice and a hearing, no matter how clear the violation, nor how convincing the evidence, nor how heinous the violation, nor how numerous the potential victims.[87] The matter does not even seem to be within the discretion of the court.[88] Thus, speedy relief may not be available when needed. This seems an unwarranted interference with the normal discretionary powers of an equity court.[89] On the other hand, in most cases, relief may be granted to prevent violations before they occur, because it need not be shown that violations have actually occurred to obtain such

---

82 U3C § 6.108(5).

83 U3C § 6.108, comment.

84 U3C § 6.108(1).

85 U3C § 6.108(2).

86 U3C §§ 6.110-.112.

87 U3C § 6.112.

88 The section states that "the Administrator may apply to the court for appropriate temporary relief," which would normally include temporary restraining orders. However, it then states the limitation "but only after a hearing." Since this language limits the Administrator's authority to apply to the court, it deprives him of standing to seek an order. *Id.*

89 Ordinarily a temporary restraining order is available when in the court's discretion special circumstances of need make that very special relief proper. *See* 7 J. MOORE, FEDERAL PRACTICE ¶¶ 65.05-.07 (2d ed. 1955); Inhabitants of Town of Lincolnville v. Perry, 150 Me. 113, 116-17, 104 A.2d 884, 887 (1954).

an order.[90] Thus, if the Administrator can obtain warning of potential violations and can prove "reasonable cause to believe" that they are planned, he may be able to forestall them. As usual, there is an exception to this rule concerning unconscionable agreements, for which proof of past violations is a requisite to any relief.[91]

If the Administrator has powers to stop violations through several devices, his ability to obtain redress is much more limited. He may not be able to obtain such redress at all, except for usury violations. The only provision which expressly allows him to seek such redress for aggrieved individuals enables him to demand "refunds" of "overcharges" (what once was called usury), and to penalize refusals to accede to such demands.[92] For all other violations, he has no express power to seek redress. However, if he brings a formal court action seeking to enjoin a creditor's conduct, he may also seek "other appropriate relief."[93] He faces two hurdles in seeking to use this phrase to obtain redress for individual consumers: First, what is "appropriate relief?" And second, has he standing to represent aggrieved consumers as a class? Redress under this phrase seems more plausible where the violation concerns the inclusion of void clauses, and the court is asked to enjoin the creditor from enforcing them. Thus the relief sought is still injunctive, but of broader scope; and the state is sometimes allowed to seek injunctive relief when representing private rights of action.[94]

---

90 U3C §§ 6.110-.112. Under U3C § 6.110, he may seek to restrain a creditor "from violating" the Act, and is not limited to enjoining them from continuing to violate. Under U3C § 6.111, he may likewise seek to restrain creditors "from engaging" in prohibited courses of conduct.

91 U3C § 6.111(2)(a). However, the court may restrain "unconscionable conduct" if it finds that the creditor "is likely to engage" in a course of such conduct.

An explanation for the many exceptions to the normal rules regarding unconscionable agreements and collection techniques is that the U3C draftsmen seem undecided about whether to call them violations of the Act or not. They do not appear in those parts of the U3C which create all other violations, but sanctions are provided against them. Further, the aggrieved consumer may not obtain relief, but the Administrator may. *See* text at notes 105-09 *infra*. These are strange results, and differences which do not seem to be based on any analytical distinctions. Until the draftsmen decide whether such conduct actually is to be prohibited, such anomalies will continue.

92 U3C § 6.113(1).

93 U3C § 6.110.

94 The issue of agency protection of the defrauded public by means of the injunctive process is not free from problems. It has been held that the state could not be granted a decree enjoining violations of the usury laws where it was not proved that victims of the practice were indigent or for other reasons unable to protect themselves, Nash v. State, 271 Ala. 173, 123 So. 2d 24 (1960), and that the state solicitor

However, where the violation requires a more sophisticated remedy, such as an election to rescind, the utility of this provision would depend upon local procedural rules concerning public representation of private rights of action in non-injunctive proceedings.[95] As long as the Administrator cannot bring a class action representing consumers, and the U3C gives him no such powers, he probably cannot obtain such rescission or reformation of contracts to which he is not a party. Thus, in many jurisdictions he may be unable to help the consumers aggrieved through the use of balloon notes, referral sales, or unauthorized home solicitation sale techniques.[96] Further, he has no ability to obtain any redress for unconscionable contracts or collection techniques, because injunctions against such practices are provided in a separate section which does not allow the court to grant "other appropriate relief."[97] Thus the Administrator literally cannot help the individual consumer who has been harassed by all-night telephone calls. As to reimbursement for his own costs

---

general was not the proper party to seek such an injunction where the duty to see that state laws are enforced was expressly vested in the governor. State *ex rel.* Boykin v. Ball Investment Co., 191 Ga. 382, 12 S.E.2d 574 (1940). *See generally,* Annot. 83 A.L.R.2d 848 (1962).

This analytical problem is compounded by the conflicting principles in the administrative law area that a delegation of power carries with it the implied powers necessary to perform the designated duty and that any delegation of authority to an administrator must be strictly construed to prevent overreaching. *Compare* discussion in United States v. Jones, 204 F.2d 745, 750-54 (7th Cir. 1953) *with* statement in United States v. Foster, 131 F.2d 3, 7 (8th Cir. 1942) that "while officers are presumed to have acted within their authority, statutes delegating powers to public officers must be strictly construed. . . ."

95 The problem here is that statutes providing for private redress through public prosecution are read narrowly. *See, e.g.,* Railroad Commissioners v. Atlantic Coast Line R. Co., 56 Fla. 525, 47 So. 870 (1908). (The Railroad Commissioner was authorized to bring a restitutional suit at request and on behalf of a private party, but his authority was read to be limited to bringing suit only in those situations peculiarly related to the duty of a common carrier). See note 94 *supra.*

96 These problems may represent one difficulty with what the draftsmen term "self-executing remedies." U3C § 2.405 gives the balloon note victim a right to refinance. Even if this were an appropriate remedy (*see* text following note 144 *infra*) a court order may be needed to obtain the refinancing from a creditor who would violate the clear provisions of the statutory section. If the Administrator may not seek such an order, and the consumer can obtain no award from the creditor for the violation, there is no risk in a violation. A court order is even more necessary where the violation involves an unauthorized home solicitation sale, because of the evidentiary problems involved, and the fact that an ineffectual cancellation is a default. As to referral sales, *see* Part II, C, *infra.*

97 U3C § 6.111. *See* note 91 *supra.*

of investigation and prosecution of the violating creditor, the U3C gives the Administrator no powers of redress. Thus, such costs must be borne by the public at large, rather than by the creditor who caused the expenditures by his own illegal acts.

If halting violations after they begin may be delayed, and redress for past violations may be unavailable, can the Administrator deter potential violations before they begin? Since the U3C does not provide for declaratory orders, so that creditors cannot determine in advance whether a proposed course of conduct will be considered a violation, the deterrent function is not emphasized. The Administrator is given two types of civil actions to recover a penalty: one for usury violations, the other for almost all types of violations. A usurer is subject to a penalty only if he refuses to refund upon demand,[98] or has deliberately violated the act.[99] The first action is designed only to deter litigation, since the violating creditor can escape the penalty by settling. The second action would seem practically unavailable because of the impossibility of proving the requisite intent, except for the self-confessed loan shark. Thus there is no penalty attaching to the simple act of charging usurious rates from time to time, not even a slight one.[100] The creditor literally risks nothing by such conduct.

A separate cause of action is given the Administrator to recover a civil penalty of up to five thousand dollars for any "repeated and willful" violation of the Act,[101] except the making of unconscionable contracts or use of unconscionable debt collection tactics.[102] Since the violations must be both repeated *and* willful, proof of a number of violations is probably insufficient. Instead, the Administrator seemingly must prove that the creditor has engaged in a "practice" of "knowingly" violating the statute.[103] In all cases, the intent requirement creates fact issues, and thereby reduces the effectiveness of the

---

98 U3C § 6.113(1).

99 U3C § 6.113(2). The penalty may be assessed if the excess charge was "in deliberate violation or in reckless disregard of" the Act. However, no penalty may be levied if the violation was "unintentional." U3C § 6.113(4). This seems to create a conflict as to reckless, but unintentional, conduct.

100 The only sanction attaching to "getting caught" at such a violation is that the overcharge must be refunded. U3C § 6.113(1). But the money refunded is all illegal profit anyway, so the creditor has at this time risked none of the funds to which he had a rightful claim.

101 U3C § 6.113(3), (4). Presumably, this sanction is available against usurers too. U3C § 6.113, comment.

102 See note 91 *supra*.

103 U3C § 6.113, comment.

deterrent because of the uncertainty of the result of the litigation. It also allows the creditor to be extremely careless in his observation of the regulatory provisions without risk. Whenever the statutory meaning is unclear or subject to several interpretations, the creditor may automatically opt for the most favorable meaning without risk.[104]

Even the dedicated, well-financed, "ombudsman-type" Administrator will have problems with this set of enforcement tools. Every action is excessively formalized. If he seeks to halt violations after they have occurred, at least formal agency proceedings are necessitated. If he seeks to prevent or deter their occurrence, or to redress the effect of past violations, he must proceed in court. As to providing redress to aggrieved consumers, this requirement virtually eliminates the effectiveness of the Administrator in providing consistent and comprehensive relief. On the other hand, the unaggressive or underfinanced civil servant can easily go through the motions without accomplishing anything. He can issue cease and desist orders whenever he happens upon a violation and accept assurances of discontinuance for later violations; believing in good faith that some day, before the statute of limitations runs, an assistant attorney general will appear and bring all the appropriate actions for all the violations in his files. The latter type of Administrator creates an immediate need for effective private enforcement, and in particular for effective provisions for redress to the aggrieved individual. Does Article 5 of the U3C so provide?

## B. *Private Enforcement Under the U3C*

In one of the most crucial areas, the U3C gives the consumer no powers to do anything—to halt, deter or seek redress for violations. Unconscionable debt collection practices are supposedly regulated by the U3C, but they are not expressly prohibited or declared

---

104 The provision, and the problems it creates, illustrate another reason for authorizing the issuance of declaratory orders.

Criminal penalty provisions are provided, but only for violations concerning misdisclosure, usury, the unlicensed making of regulated loans, and non-notification to the administrator of engaging in consumer financing. U3C §§ 5.301-.02. No criminal penalties are provided which apply to any other violations of the act, no matter how heinous. The draftsmen may have underrated the effect of such sanctions, even if prosecutions are not brought. *See* note 43 *supra.* License revocations are also possible if the violating creditor is authorized to make "regulated loans." U3C § 3.504. The criterion for revocation is the same as that for imposing a civil penalty. *Compare* U3C § 3.504(1)(a) *with* U3C § 6.113(3). Thus it possesses the same faults.

a violation.[105] Thus, the consumer has no right of action under the statute against the creditor who uses such tactics. Even though a remedy for such unconscionable conduct is developing in tort,[106] the U3C provides that the creditor's rights on the contract may not be impaired by such conduct.[107] The broad language of the U3C may even jeopardize the development of the tort action, because the U3C expressly undertakes to regulate such conduct and refuses the debtor a remedy.[108] Has it preempted the field?[109] There is no reason either to deny the consumer a remedy through private action, or to create doubts concerning the validity of the developing tort remedy. The aggrieved consumer is being directly affected by the conduct, and he should therefore be able to act on his own initiative, without regard to the Administrator's finances or philosophy. The draftsmen of a modern consumer protection statute should recognize the modern tort developments and incorporate them into the U3C.

As to the halting of violations, the consumer has no express power to seek injunctions under the U3C, so that he will have difficulties attempting to halt them, even through a class action. The difficulties arise because the relief is too limited if the class comprises only past victims, but potential victims as a class may not yet have standing to sue.[110] Thus the statute would have to expressly grant

---

105 U3C § 6.111. Unconscionable agreements and clauses also are not labelled as violations, but courts are permitted to refuse to enforce them, regardless of the parties to the action. U3C § 5.106. Presumably, such language will create a right of action in equity for reformation in most states. *See* text at note 133 *infra*.

106 Three principles currently being used in the abusive debt collection technique area are: the right of privacy, Norris v. Moskin Stores, Inc., 272 Ala. 174, 132 So. 2d 321 (1961); the intentional infliction of emotional distress, Lyons v. Zale Jewelry Co., 246 Miss. 139, 150 So. 2d 154 (1963); and unreasonable collection practices, Signature Indorsement Co. v. Wilson, 392 S.W.2d 484 (Tex. Civ. App. 1965). *See* Note, *Mental Distress From Collection Activities*, 17 HASTINGS L.J. 369 (1965); Comment, *Effectively Regulating Extra-Judicial Collection of Debts*, 20 ME. L. REV. 261 (1968); Comment, *Collection Capers: Liability for Debt Collection Practices*, 24 U. CHI. L. REV. 572 (1957).

107 U3C § 5.201(1).

108 The counter argument is that the U3C seeks only to regulate contract remedies, not those for breach of common law duties. However, the U3C ignores standard contract measures of damage throughout.

109 *Cf., e.g.*, Lonzrick v. Republic Steel Corp., 6 Ohio St. 2d 227, 240-52, 218 N.E.2d 185, 194-201 (1966) (dissenting opinion).

110 While a victim should be allowed to seek an injunction against a prohibited course of conduct, an as yet uninjured member of the consuming public would not be permitted to sue for failure to show the requisite special injury different from that suffered by the general public. *See, e.g.*, G. T. McGovern Trucking Co. v. Moses, 92 N.Y.S.2d 550 (Sup. Ct. 1949).

It is even questionable whether a private consumer could, under the U3C, obtain

standing to seek an injunction, and it does not. If the consumer is to have any ability to prevent violations, it must therefore come through the technique of deterring future violations by penalizing such conduct after it has occurred.

For most violations of the act, the U3C provides no potential deterrent through private actions, because the aggrieved consumer may not recover any penalty award. Penalties are available only where the violation concerns usury, misdisclosure, referral sales, regulated loan payments schedules, or the making of regulated loans without a license.[111] There are no penalties, as such, attached to such other violations as use of negotiable promissory notes, balloon notes and clauses assigning earnings, confessing judgment, waiving defenses, providing unreasonable attorneys fees and default charges, and unconscionable debt collection techniques.[112] Thus neither an individual consumer, nor any conscientious group of consumers, can even attempt to deter such conduct through private enforcement. Even if void, their *in terrorem* use is a major abuse, and consumers should be able to deter it on their own initiative.

Even in cases of usury, the deterrent effect available through private action is nonexistent. No penalty is available if the creditor refunds the usurious charge upon demand.[113] The creditor must not only violate the statute, but also refuse redress in order to be penalized. Therefore, the penalty does not seek to deter the violation itself, but only the refusal to furnish redress after violation.[114] This is the only section which seeks to deter litigation; all other sections provide no additional award if the creditor compels the consumer to undertake its hazards.

Most of the penalties which are provided are related to a cancellation of "loan finance charge" or the "credit service charge"

---

injunctive relief since that function is expressly vested in the Administrator (U3C § 6.110) and where the legislature has designated certain parties to perform a certain function, parties not included may be deemed excluded. *Cf.* New York Post Corp. v. Moses, 10 N.Y.2d 199, 176 N.E.2d 709 (1961). *See* notes 49 *supra,* and 133 *infra.*

111 U3C §§ 5.201(2)-(5), 5.202(1).

112 U3C §§ 2.403-.415, 3.402-.407, 3.512, 3.604, 6.111. The U3C does in some cases provide some relief for such violations, but the creditor never is required to give up more than his ill-gotten gains in such circumstances. *See* text at notes 52ff. *supra* and at notes 127ff. *infra.*

113 U3C § 5.201(3). There is a penalty available if the violation was "deliberate," even if the overcharge is refunded upon demand. However, the burden of proof of the *mens rea* would seem to be on the consumer, which effectively eliminates the utility of the exception in practice. *Compare* § 5.201(6).

114 *See* text following note 57 *supra.*

(both of which are hereafter called "interest").[115] The penalties available for violations of referral sales and regulated loan schedules are so highly conditioned that they are probably not effective either. The penalty available is the cancellation of the interest charge.[116] This penalty is available whether the matter is settled out of court or litigated. Thus there is no inducement to the creditor to settle out of court rather than to threaten litigation and hope the consumer will not accept the risks it entails. However, the award, in all cases, is conditioned upon a finding that the creditor's violation was intentional.[117] It therefore does not provide absolute liability, and does not seek to deter careless violations.[118] Even the deterrent to the culpable violator is probably ineffective. The award is conditioned on intent and the presence of an interest charge which is clearly identifiable as such.[119] With these conditions upon its availability, it is very unlikely that the penalty will be available in any practical sense without litigation.[120] But the award provided is probably too small to induce a consumer to undertake the risks and expenses of litigation, especially if appeals are possible.

The remedies provided for misdisclosure are the same as in the

---

[115] The linguistic distinctions between "loan finance charge" and "credit service charge" in current use are due to the time-price doctrine and are conceptually difficult to rationalize. An attack upon so ancient a concept as the time-price doctrine is outside the scope of this article. The distinction between the credit sale and cash loan will probably continue to be made, but only because of policy reasons based on the modern economics of consumer credit, and the requirements of usury statutes adopted without such economics in mind. Therefore, because this article is concerned with the enforceability of any type of provision limiting rates of return on loans, the circumlocutions of the doctrine will be ignored, as will distinctions based *solely* on the status of the creditor as a lender or a merchant. *See* Hare v. General Contract Purchase Corp., 220 Ark. 601, 249 S.W.2d 973 (1952); Littlefield, *Parties and Transactions Covered by Consumer-Credit Legislation*, 8 B.C. IND. & COMM. L. REV. 463 (1967).

[116] U3C § 5.201(4).

[117] U3C § 5.201(6). Although the statute is much more circumloquacious, through assigning the burden of proof on the issue to the creditor, the result is the same. The statute requires the court to decide whether the violation was intentional or not, and only if this question is decided in the debtor's favor is the added sanction available.

[118] *See* text at note 64 *supra.*

[119] The effect of this condition on the award in referral sale violation is remarkable. *See* text at notes 143-44 *infra.*

[120] It would be extremely unwise for the consumer even merely to stop payment of interest without the protection of a court order or a written release by the creditor. No matter how obvious the violation, it could always be claimed to be unintentional, freeing the creditor from liability for the penalty and automatically placing the unprotected consumer in default on his obligation. This will be very tricky for the layman unless guided by counsel at every step.

federal Truth in Lending Act.[121] They provide a slightly greater penalty award, twice the interest charges, up to one thousand dollars. Further, there is a minimum liability of one hundred dollars, regardless of the amount of interest. The award is more certain than others provided by the U3C. It is mandatory for all misdisclosure violations, if made "knowingly." There is a presumption that any violation was made knowingly, and the creditor must prove not only that the misdisclosure was the result of a bona fide error but also that he maintained procedures which were reasonably adapted to avoid such an error.[122]

The only violation for which both principal and interest may be cancelled is the making of "regulated loans" without a license.[123] However, this penalty also seems illusory. The distinction between regulated loans and others is the greater interest rate allowed the regulated lender—he may charge more than 10 per cent per year.[124] Therefore, the creditor who charges more than that may claim that he is merely a usurer, not an unlicensed regulated lender, and that he is liable for no more than the lesser usury penalties.

Thus the consumer probably has no effective deterrent powers against any volations of his statutory rights. For most violations he simply is given no deterrent power by the statute. Against two violations, usury and unlicensed regulated lending, the express deterrent provided seems illusory. While the deterrent available against referral sales and unauthorized schedules in regulated loans is not entirely illusory, it is so small, and so highly qualified, that it is unlikely to be available in practice. The deterrent available against misdisclosure is also subject to the same objections, but to a lesser extent. However, in the last case, the remedial provisions in the U3C have been literally forced upon the draftsmen by Congress.[125]

If the consumer cannot stop the recurrence of violations, and cannot deter their occurrence, can he at least obtain redress when he discovers that his rights have been violated? This question is of crucial importance, since the Administrator himself probably cannot obtain such redress in many instances. The answer to this

---

121 *Compare* 82 Stat. 146, § 130(a)(1), 1968 *United States Code, Cong. and Admin. News* 1232, 1245 *with* U3C § 5.202(1). The amount of the award is the same whether litigation is required or not, so that there is no deterrent to the creditor refusing to negotiate.

122 U3C § 5.202(2).

123 U3C § 5.201(5).

124 U3C §§ 3.201, 3.501.

125 *See* note 121 *supra.*

question depends upon what one considers to be "redress" when the consumer's rights have been violated. If redress is considered to be the refunding of a usurious charge or the striking of a prohibited clause from the contract, it is sometimes available. However, if redress is considered also to include compensation for the consumer's investment of his time, money and reputation, this is not available under the U3C. Attorney's fees may be awarded, at the court's discretion,[126] but this does not compensate for other investments. Nor does reimbursement for actual expenditures, if successful, provide an incentive to undertake the risks of litigation. Further, the attorney's fees are reimbursed only when litigation is required.[127] Thus there is no inducement to the consumer to seek counsel when attempting to settle out of court, so that he will probably exercise unauthorized self-help and create all the problems caused thereby. Article 5 therefore ignores a prominent known problem.[128]

If the consumer is not afforded redress in the sense of full compensation, he should at least be given relief from the injurious effects of the creditor's violation. Under the U3C, however, such relief is not always available. It sometimes allows only the Administrator to act against wrongful conduct, and then fails to provide him the power to obtain any compensation for the aggrieved consumer.[129] In other circumstances, the relief which is provided is completely irrelevant to the injury caused by the creditor's violation. The relief provided by the U3C may conveniently be divided into four categories: (1) refund of a usurious charge,[130] which seems appropriate if full redress is not to be provided; (2) a right to cancel the contract,[131] which also seems appropriate; (3) a statutory prohibition against certain devices, sometimes with a declaration that

---

126 U3C § 5.201(7). Attorney's fees "may" be granted by the court, not "shall" be granted, but no standards are set to guide the court's discretion.

127 *Id.* The consumer has a right to such fees only if they are awarded by a court, presupposing a litigation context.

128 It has been suggested to the draftsmen that the entire statutory scheme will not provide protection to poor consumers unless a default after a creditor violation is recognized at least to the extent of not depriving the defaulting consumer of all rights under the contract. Nat'l Legal Aid and Defender Ass'n, Joint Statement of NLDA and OEO Legal Services Program Re Working Draft No. 6 of UCCC, at 4 (January 10, 1968). This author cannot, however, find any attempt in the U3C to deal with this problem.

129 For such wrongs, the consumer must rely upon a non-statutory tort cause of action. See text at notes 98 and 107-110 *supra.*

130 U3C § 5.201(2).

131 U3C § 2.502.

the device is void if used, which is rarely appropriate; and (4) cancellation of the interest charge, which is rarely appropriate where used.

The statute's major reliance is on the third method of relief listed; prohibition and voiding of devices which have been abused by creditors in the past. This relief is provided for wage assignments, confession of judgment clauses, clauses providing for unreasonable attorney's fees and default charges, encumbrance of all the consumer's property, waivers of defenses (one alternative only), and promissory notes (no voiding, however).[132] The limitations on the value of such relief where third parties are involved should be obvious. For example: (1) The holder of the promissory note must still be paid, greatly reducing the consumer's negotiating position with a defaulting seller. (2) The consumer must still explain to his employer that the wage assignment is unenforceable, or more likely procure a court order protecting the employer so as not to jeopardize his job.

Even where only two parties are involved, the value of the relief is questionable. Although many of the devices are termed void, this will not defeat their *in terrorem* use. What is appropriate relief to the consumer when a creditor asserts a right to collateral under a void contract clause? Some form of court action is required, probably a declaratory judgment and a restraining order against enforcing the clause. Thus the statute should provide, not only for such an action, but also for reimbursement to him for his litigation risks and expenses. The U3C does not expressly provide for such an action, although courts will probably create one through normal equity powers.[133] The statute does provide for discretionary recovery of reasonable attorney's fees, in litigation only, "in any case in which it is found that a creditor is liable for a violation of this act."[134] However, since no express right of action is conferred on the consumer aggrieved by a prohibited contract clause, and therefore no express creditor liability is created, he may have no right to reimbursement for such fees, even if he must litigate to achieve redress. His right to reimbursement depends upon the construction of *"liable* for a viola-

---

132 U3C §§ 2.403-.415, 3.402-.407, 3.512, 3.604.

133 Drafting history could be dangerous here. Working Draft No. 4 provided an express right of action against all violations, U3C (Working Draft No. 4, 1967) § 5.201(3). This has since been eliminated. Does this elimination create an argument that these violations are only matters of defense, and not proper subjects of declaratory judgment actions or actions to reform contracts?

134 U3C § 5.201(7).

tion of this act." It may refer to all violations for which a court will order relief, or it may only refer to those violations which create express liability under the statute. The latter construction limits recovery to the five violations specified in U3C sections 5.201 and 5.202. In any case, the statute should not be so unclear as to require subsequent litigation over the recovery of earlier litigation expenses.

Cancellation of interest charges is inappropriate as the sole relief for unconscionable debt collection techniques, because injuries can vary from nominal to extremely severe. For such violations, tort damages are the only measure which can provide appropriate compensation for the injuries received. Another situation in which cancellation of interest is inappropriate is when the violation concerns an inducement to the consumer to contract. In such circumstances, rescission seems more appropriate to protect the consumer's expectations.

C. *An Illustration of the U3C in Operation*

Let us take, as a possible example of the effectiveness of the U3C's enforcement provisions, the referral sale transaction in which a discount is offered if referrals subsequently buy from seller. The draftsmen attempted to abolish this device, expressly stating that no one may offer to make such a sale.[135] But suppose someone does, what can anyone do about it?

The Administrator may seek to prevent this course of dealing, or to halt it once it has begun. He may approach the problem either through a cease and desist order or a civil action for an injunction. Both approaches are formal and eventually depend upon court orders, so that notice and hearing are prerequisites to any permanent relief. Even temporary relief is greatly delayed, regardless of the circumstances. The U3C makes notice and hearing mandatory before issuance of a temporary restraining order, in contrast to normal equity practice. The length of notice required is not specified, but he may not seek court enforcement of cease and desist orders until 30 days after the agency hearing and the issuance of the agency order. Thus delays may be lengthy indeed, making agency proceedings unsuitable for the mass violation situation. The scope of the order provided through the agency proceeding also seems limited, since it can prohibit only past practices and may not apply to similar, but slightly different, violations.

No informal method of handling such violations is expressly

---

[135] U3C § 2.411.

authorized. Thus the halting of each violation requires large expenditures of resources, especially attorney's time. Nor is the Administrator reimbursed for any of these expenditures, as such, even when the creditor is proved to have violated the statute.

If the Administrator cannot quickly halt violations of the statute, he must rely heavily on his ability to deter them through penalties. However, in order to recover any deterrent penalty under the U3C, he must prove that the creditor willfully *and* repeatedly violated the statute.[136] Proof of several violations may be insufficient, because of the willfulness requirement; and proof of a consistent course of dealing may be required, according to the Comment.[137] Thus, the creditor who is careful enough to make such sales only from time to time is arguably not subject to any penalty. In practice, this would require the Administrator to allow many violations to occur, establishing a practice, before he would consider his evidence sufficient to seek a penalty. Such a deterrent provision is of little practical utility, because the Administrator should not be willing to delay prosecution until such a practice is established.

The Administrator is especially unlikely to wait as violations occur when he knows that he is powerless to provide any redress to aggrieved individuals under the U3C. There is no express authority for him to bring an action to seek such redress, or even to negotiate with the creditor on behalf of the aggrieved consumer. The only possible avenue for attempting redress is U3C section 6.110 which permits an action for an injunction "and other appropriate relief." Even if he can persuade a court that redress to aggrieved consumers would be an appropriate relief, he probably still cannot succeed. The court cannot impair the creditor's contract rights except as "otherwise provided" by the statute.[138] The only such provision creates a right of action in the consumer to cancel the contractual interest charge.[139] But the statute gives the Administrator no standing to represent consumers, even in a class action for redress; so he may not have standing to seek such cancellations, and therefore no ability to obtain any redress for individuals.

The consumer's rights to enforce the statute are even more limited. He has no power to seek to enjoin the violations. Instead, the statutory remedy provided him for all purposes is the cancella-

---

136 U3C § 6.113(3).
137 U3C § 6.113, comment.
138 U3C § 5.201(1).
139 U3C § 5.201(4).

tion of the interest charge.[140] However, the consumer would be well-advised to obtain either a court order or a written release admitting the intentional nature of the violation before failing to pay interest. Otherwise, he may be in default if a court later finds that the violation was unintentional.[141] This requires an investment in legal fees, with or without litigation; and the resulting award seems insufficient to induce the undertaking of such expenses when coupled with the risks of litigation.[142]

Further, a creditor who wishes to avoid private actions, *and any redress*, may easily do so by simply raising his cash price and eliminating the express interest charge. The remedy available would then be the striking of the conditional discount provisions from the contract, leaving the remainder of the contract enforceable without impairment,[143] including the original sale price. This seems a strange result, and indicates that the draftsmen have not yet thought the problem through. One solution to this problem is to provide a minimum recovery, as in the federal Truth in Lending Act.[144]

However, the minimum recovery does not solve the deeper problems created by the inappropriate relation of the injuries to the cancellation of the interest charge. The referral sale is prohibited because of its capacity to defraud the consumer by inducing unwarranted expectations of large discounts which will usually not be realized. There is no necessary relationship between these asserted discounts and the interest charge, so that there is no relation between the consumer's loss of expectations and the damages provided by the statute. It can usually be presumed that the consumer would not have purchased from the particular seller without the supposed discounts, so the appropriate remedy to protect his expectations is rescission. Further, this remedy is appropriate whenever the violation concerns a prohibited inducement to form the contract, such as misrepresentation of the cash price, interest rate or payment schedule, including the use of the balloon note.[145]

---

140 *Id.*

141 U3C § 5.201(6)(b). *See* text at notes 63-64 *supra.*

142 *See* text at notes 58-60 *supra.*

143 U3C § 5.201(1).

144 *See* note 121 *supra.*

145 Contrast the remedy available under U3C § 2.405, which provides mandatory refinancing of a balloon payment. The remedy assumes that the consumer desires to refinance, which may not in fact be correct if he was induced to contract because low weekly payments were quoted and were available only because of the balloon. What is an appropriate remedy if the last payment is equal to the original principal, so that the consumer must make payments forever?

The referral sale illustrates the difficulties of enforcing the U3C. The Administrator realistically has the power only to enjoin violations. He faces difficult problems of proving intent if he seeks to impose a penalty, and seems barred from seeking redress through a class action or otherwise. Any possible recovery by the consumer is both uncertain and inappropriate. Thus it can neither deter violations nor provide redress related to the injuries suffered. Perhaps the public is better protected by the ambiguities of the present law which permits such sales to be attacked as frauds[146] or as illegal lotteries[147] with potent remedies available to the aggrieved consumer.[148]

### III. SUGGESTED CHANGES

Any analysis of a statute involves an evaluation on two different levels: (1) the policy decisions made by the draftsmen, and (2) the drafting techniques used to implement them. Often it is very difficult to differentiate the two. However, one policy decision of the U3C draftsmen stands out clearly—they seek to provide a "strong" Administrator who will aggressively protect the consumer and assume an ombudsman role.[149] This seems a wise decision and necessary in the present credit economy.[150] A second policy decision is also apparent—private enforcement has been rigidly limited, sufficiently so to defeat its effectiveness. This decision cannot be logically supported. Limitations on private enforcement are not necessary to provide a strong Administrator, nor to enhance his powers. He can protect effectively without having enforcement powers vested exclusively in him. If it is the result of a compromise among the draftsmen, the consumers' need for alternative methods of enforcement in states traditionally having underfinanced or unaggressive

---

146 *See, e.g.,* Norman v. World Wide Distrib. Inc., 202 Pa. Super. 53, 195 A.2d 115 (1963).

147 *See, e.g.,* Sherwood & Roberts-Yakima, Inc. v. Leach, 67 Wash. 2d 630, 409 P.2d 160 (1965).

148 *See* authorities cited in notes 146-47 *supra.* In *Norman,* the court voided a prior judgment held by the creditor and ordered rescission of the purchase agreement, directing the buyer to return the goods. In *Leach,* the court held the purchase agreement unenforceable and rendered a summary judgment against the creditor when it sued for the purchase price. Such remedies are both more potent and more appropriate for the misled consumer than cancelling the interest charge.

149 NATIONAL CONFERENCE OF COMMISSIONERS ON UNIFORM STATE LAWS, REPORT OF SPECIAL COMMITTEE ON RETAIL INSTALLMENT SALES, CONSUMER CREDIT, SMALL LOANS AND USURY 37 (1965).

150 *See* text at notes 5-8 *supra.*

administrators has been ignored.[151] A Uniform Act should be flexible enough to operate effectively in different bureaucratic climates. Thus, this basic policy decision should be reconsidered.

## A.  The Administrator's Powers

Even if the Administrator has all the personal characteristics sought by the draftsmen, he has not been given sufficient powers to exercise control easily and efficiently. The draftsmen have concentrated primarily on giving him tools to halt violations, or enjoin them. The other possible enforcement tools have not received equal emphasis, resulting in a slighting of the deterrent function and omission of redress capabilities. Further, there seems a preference for formality which has resulted in the elimination of informal enforcement devices. This requires the Administrator either to ignore some violations or to escalate the conflict into the courts, an unnecessary drain on his resources. It also slows down his speed of reaction to serious violations. He needs a variety of powers to meet the countless subtly different situations which will arise. The following suggestions therefore accept the basic U3C policy of creating an Administrator with strong powers, and seek to improve the efficiency and ease with which he may enforce the U3C's regulatory provisions.

First, he should be given the power to issue declaratory orders, which he presently does not have. This would provide creditors information about agency beliefs, and a method of testing those beliefs without violating the statute to obtain approval of specific proposed courses of conduct without risking consumer good will. The creditor could place more reliance upon such an order than upon informal advice, although they should be subject to reversal by courts or rescission by the Administrator.[152]

Second, he should have the power to accept assurances of discontinuance for first violations by a creditor, so that he may deal with these violations in an informal manner if he so chooses. The present draft allows use of this device only after an agency or a court order is in force against a creditor. This limitation on the availability of the device is a change from prior drafts,[153] and there

---

151 *See* text at notes 9-16 *supra.*

152 *See* note 25 *supra.*

153 U3C § 6.109 (Working Draft No. 4, 1967). The prior draft permitted use of the assurance against practices "which *could be* restrained by the Administrator . . . or a court. . . ." (emphasis added.) The use of the conditional language obviated any necessity that the practice be already subject to an administrative or court order when the assurance is accepted.

seems to be no reason for the limitation. Further, the power of the Administrator to attach conditions to his acceptance of the assurance should be expressly stated, so that he may require redress to consumers, reimbursement for investigation expenses, admissions of past violations, and establishment of escrow funds to cover costs of future violations in return for his decision not to initiate more formal proceedings.[154] With such an enforcement tool, many cases could be processed cheaply, allowing more efficient use of agency resources.

Third, the Administrator should be enabled to issue orders of broader scope through agency proceedings than under the present draft. Although it is necessary to be able to issue cease and desist orders, the effectiveness of the agency proceeding would be greatly enhanced if it could also provide resolution of problems relating, for example, to redress for aggrieved individuals. Some mechanical drafting problems also need attention. Must the court issue an enforcement order if the Administrator makes the showing required in section 6.108(5), or is this discretionary?[155] Can defenses be interposed by the creditor at this point?

Fourth, the Administrator must be able to act quickly to restrain violations where there is evidence of irreparable, immediate harm threatened to large segments of the population. Thus he must be able to seek a temporary restraining order without notice or hearing when appropriate.[156] Equity courts are well-equipped to determine whether prior hearings should be required, and the express limitation on the Administrator's power under the U3C seems an unnecessary interference with their normal discretionary powers.

Fifth, the Administrator has no express powers to seek redress for individual aggrieved consumers. If the draftsmen believe that few consumers will act affirmatively to seek such redress, and do not promote actions by them, the Administrator must be able to bring such actions or a vacuum may be created. The most feasible solution to this problem is to provide expressly that he may represent consumers and bring class actions in their name to obtain any relief

---

154 Detailed rules need not be established, although this seems preferable and examples exist. *See* notes 28 & 29 *supra*. The objective could also be achieved by permitting the Administrator to set any "reasonable" conditions on his acceptance of the assurance. *See* UCC § 2-609(2).

155 The reference is to the second sentence of U3C § 6.108(5). *See* text at note 82 *supra*.

156 He should also be able to seize and condemn any forms or advertising matter which do not comply with the statute. *See* note 36 *supra*.

available to them, including rescission and cancellation of contracts. He should also have power to obtain redress for himself, through reimbursement for investigation expenses. Where a creditor has in fact violated the statute, the costs of processing the violation should be borne by the creditor, not the general public. Such redress will also induce the creditor not to attempt to exhaust the Administrator's resources by endless appeals. Redress to both the aggrieved consumer and the Administrator should be available without regard to the creditor's intent in committing the violation.

Sixth, the Administrator should have greater powers to seek to penalize violations after occurrence, and thereby deter them before occurrence. If declaratory orders are available, provision of an absolute liability standard for civil penalties should be reconsidered by the draftsmen. Even if this standard is not adopted, the present standard, requiring proof of both repeated violations *and* willfulness, is too severe. The intent requirement allows the "white-hearted" creditor to proceed without attempting to ascertain the requirements of a statute regulating his business. Surely, if the statute is to have any meaning, the creditor who carelessly ignores it should be subject to sanction. Thus penalties should be available for violations which are either repeated *or* willful.[157]

Seventh, the whole range of enforcement devices available to process other violations should also be available to act against unconscionable debt collection techniques. The present provisions, which require formal court proceedings in all circumstances, can only inhibit understanding of the concept, and prolong the creditor's uneasiness at being subject to unknown requirements. The Administrator should be able to furnish information, including declaratory judgments, about the agency's beliefs as to its scope. He should also be able to process such violations through agency proceedings, to foster agency expertise in analyzing the definitional problems.

## B. *Effective Private Enforcement*

The present draft of the U3C rigidly limits the enforcement powers of the individual consumer through private action. However, under such a policy, the consumer has no protection in a state

---

157 The draftsmen should also reconsider their deletion of criminal sanctions for most violations. Such sanctions may provide a powerful deterrent, even if not used, because the violation can then never be considered only a risk of money, for which accountants may calculate the odds. *See* note 43 *supra*.

in which the Administrator is dominated by the industry, personally unaggressive, or simply underfinanced from public funds. Thus the following suggestions do not accept the basic U3C policy and seek to provide effective private enforcement where there presently is none.

First, the consumer's right of action against unconscionable collection techniques should not be left in doubt. If he *ever* needs the ability to act on his own initiative, without hinderance from administrative inertia, it is when he is being harassed by all-night telephone calls or his job is in jeopardy. There are tort theories which are developing to deal with such situations. But if the U3C regulates this conduct through administrative action only, the growth or even availability of these doctrines may be limited. Thus the statute should either undertake to provide an effective statutory cause of action to redress such unconscionable conduct, or should expressly disclaim any intention to limit the development of the tort doctrines. It would seem preferable to deal with the problem in a consumer protection statute, but only if it is possible to forge as strong a remedy as will eventually be created by case law, including recovery of all damages available in tort actions. If this is not politically possible, development should remain in the judicial forum, but without any interference from the statute.

Second, the statute should provide an express right of action to redress all violations of its provisions. Earlier working drafts so provided,[158] and there is no reason for the change in Working Draft No. 6. The attempt at creating "self-executing remedies" has in turn created at least two unnecessary problems. Even if the courts will recognize actions for reformation of the contract or declaratory judgment in such circumstances, and do not limit such remedies to defenses only,[159] they can only strike a void clause. Thus they cannot afford the consumer complete redress for the violation, but only relief from its injurious effects. Additionally, the self-executing remedies concept has led the draftsmen to formulate inappropriate remedies in some situations, and remedies which are enforceable only

---

158 U3C § 5.201(3) (Working Draft No. 4, 1967). Further, courts should be allowed more flexibility in designing appropriate remedies. Thus U3C § 5.201(1) seems unwise, because it expressly limits the court to the statutory formulation, whether effective or not, and whether appropriate or not. If it were deleted, courts could exercise a useful discretion to adapt the remedy to the numerous different types of fact patterns which will be presented.

159 *See* note 133 *supra.* Another problem is the recovery of attorney's fees by the successful consumer litigant. *See* text following note 133 *supra.*

through court orders in others.[160] Thus, if Working Draft No. 6 proves anything, it is that effective private enforcement must start from an express grant of a right of action against all violations, and the nature of the remedies may then be developed without artificial limitations.

Third, the consumer must be provided redress which fully compensates him not only for the injury caused by the violation itself but also for his actions in obtaining a correction of the violation. This concept has several ramifications. Thus, where the matter is settled out of court, the consumer must be compensated for his investment in attorney's fees and his own time and reputation in seeking the settlement. A consumer protection statute must seek to route him to an attorney, and a necessary inducement is that he not be economically penalized for seeking such counsel. This requires that he receive, through a negotiated settlement, not only a refund of an overcharge or the striking of a void clause, but also an additional award to compensate him for acting. The award suggested herein is a stated dollar amount related to a typical attorney's fee or cancellation of the interest charge, whichever is greater. However, where the violation created a false inducement to contract, such an award is entirely inappropriate, because the consumer's basic expectations have been destroyed. The only relief which will protect his expectations is rescission, and it should be optionally available in all such circumstances.

Where a violating creditor refuses to settle, compelling litigation, the investments of time and money are greatly increased, so the compensation for them must be greater. Also, the award given the successful consumer litigant must recognize the uncertainties of litigation and increase the award both to compensate him for undertaking such risks and to induce him to do so. Without such inducements, the test cases necessary to clarify the statute, and to develop new theories to conform to changing social concepts, may never be brought. The proper award to achieve such results would seem to be a voiding of the obligation, both as to principal and interest.

No compensatory award should depend upon the willfulness of the creditor in causing the violation. Conditioning the award on intent misconceives its purpose, and introduces an irrelevant deterrent analysis. The lesser awards for negotiated settlements are

---

160 *E.g.,* the balloon note: U3C §§ 2.405, 3.402, *see* note 145 *supra;* and the wage assignment: U3C §§ 2.410, 3.403, *see* text following note 132 *supra.*

primarily compensatory and only incidentally a deterrent. The increase in the awards to a successful litigant serves multiple purposes. It compensates for expenses, especially awards of attorney's fees; it provides incentive to the consumer to undertake litigation risks; and it promotes negotiated settlements by deterring litigation. Even its deterrent function relates only to the creditor's decision to compel litigation, not to his decision to commit the original violation. Thus, if he decides to compel litigation, his earlier lack of *mens rea* in violating the statute is irrelevant to increasing the award.

If the redress awards provided are fully compensatory, they will also provide a deterrent to violation enforceable through private actions. This would be available on the individual's own initiative, and could not be frustrated by agency inertia, philosophy or underfinancing. Further, this device could provide a significant deterrent. Although each award would be fairly small, the aggregate of the possible awards to all the customers of a large-volume creditor through a class action could add up to a formidable sum. In those cases where such awards would not be effective, such as a widely dispersed and diverse class, a private injunction action seems preferable to a larger award to the individual consumer. Thus, the draftsmen should reconsider their present decision not to allow such actions and determine whether an appropriately limited right in aggrieved consumers to seek such injunctions can be devised.

## IV.  CONCLUSION

The U3C, as presently drafted, does not provide for effective enforcement of its regulatory provisions. A strong, well-financed Administrator can enjoin conduct to prevent violations from reoccurring; but he cannot redress the effects of prior violations upon aggrieved consumers, and the deterrent provided is practically useless. Further, even to halt violations, court proceedings are always required, which is costly, difficult and inefficient; and there is never any reimbursement to the Administrator. Thus useful public enforcement will be provided under the U3C primarily in the larger states having large budgets for state agencies and a tradition of aggressiveness by agencies. However, all enforcement will continually be dependent upon the mood of the legislature in establishing budgets, which will limit the Administrator's independence.

In the smaller states, where "weak" and underfinanced agencies are more traditional, the U3C cannot be enforced. The expense of the formal court procedures required will preclude their use, and the informal procedures in the statute have no express teeth. The obvious answer to this lack of public enforcement is to provide for effective private enforcement, but the U3C has no such provisions. The consumer not only has no deterrent powers, but also in most circumstances cannot obtain any appropriate redress for his grievance. The draftsmen seem to have decided that consumers are inherently unable to protect themselves through private actions. This is a judgment by urban attorneys which underestimates the interest and ability of the "country lawyer" in consumer problems if there is some likelihood of some payment. It also indicates a real difference between available resources to solve problems in rural and urban settings. The Administrator is less likely to be effective in the smaller states, while private action is more likely to be effective.

Effective private enforcement depends upon the solution of two problems: The consumer must be induced to seek legal counsel; and the attorney must be paid, whether he litigates or not. The U3C attacks neither of these problems, however, which indicates to this author that the problems have not been sufficiently analyzed. There are similar problems in the public enforcement article, as is illustrated by the Administrator's lack of power to obtain redress for aggrieved individual consumers and his inability to act quickly against mass violations creating irreparable harm. Is a statute with this many problems still unsolved ready for either final adoption by Commissioners or enactment by any state?[161]

---

[161] Non-uniform amendments to Articles 5 and 6 of the U3C are another potential solution to these problems. Uniformity in the remedies sections is not necessary to achieve the purposes of the statute, as is discussed in greater depth in Spanogle, *Why Does the Proposed Uniform Consumer Credit Code Eschew Private Enforcement?*, 23 BUS. LAW. 1039, 1053-54 (1968).

# APPENDIX

Several of the thoughts in the article were incorporated into a bill presented to the Maine Legislature in 1971. (L.D. 1676, 105th Maine Legislature.) The bill was supported by consumer and merchant groups, but was withdrawn by its sponsor at the request of lender groups, especially banks. The following sections give some idea of the breadth of revision necessary to provide effective enforcement under the U3C. The new language is italicized.

§5.202. Effect of violations on rights of parties

(1) If a creditor has violated the provisions of this Act applying to *authority to make supervised loans, section 3.502, balloon payments, sections 2.405 and 3.402, referral sales or loans, sections 2.411 and 3.409, or home solicitation sales, section 2.503, the credit sale or loan is void and the debtor is not obligated to pay either the principal or credit service or loan finance charges. If he has paid any part of the principal or of the credit service or loan finance charge, he has a right to recover the payment from the person violating this Act or from an assignee of that person's rights who undertakes direct collection of payments or enforcement of rights arising from the debt.*

(2) If a creditor has violated the provisions of this Act applying to *waiver clauses, section 1.107, maximum service or loan finance charges, sections 2.201, 2.207, 3.201 and 3.508, delinquency charges, sections 2.203 and 3.203 deferral charges, sections 2.204 and 3.204, refinancing charges, sections 2.205 and 3.205, consolidation charges, sections 2.206 and 3.206, use of multiple agreements, sections 2.402 and 3.509, certain negotiable instruments, section 2.403, assignee subject to defenses, section 2.404, restrictions on liability in consumer leases, section 2.406, security in sales or leases, section 2.407, cross-collateral, section 2.408, assignments of earnings, sections 2.410 and 3.403, attorneys' fees, sections 2.413 and 3.514, limitations on default charges, sections 2.414 and 3.405, authorizations to confess judgment, sections 2.415 and 3.407, interest in land as security, section 3.510, limitations on the schedule of payments or maximum term, sections 2.211 and 3.511, excess charge for credit insurance, section 4.104, separate charges for property insurance, section 4.301, restrictions on deficiency judgments, section 5.103, garnishment before judgment, section 5.104, or limitations on garnishment, section 5.105, the debtor is entitled*

*to have the contract reformed to conform with this Act, and in addition is entitled to deduct from his total obligaion either $50 or the credit service charge or loan finance charge, whichever is greater.*

(3) *If a creditor has violated this Act and he or a transferee of his rights to whom the debt is then owing fails to offer the relief provided in subsection (2) within a reasonable time after a demand for such relief by the debtor, the obligation is void and the debtor is not obligated to pay the principal or the loan finance charge or the amount financed or the credit service charge. If the debtor has made any payments, including a down payment, he has a right to recover the payments from the person violating this Act or from a transferee of that person's rights to whom the debt is then owing.*

. . .

(5) In any case in which it is found that a creditor has violated this Act, the court *shall* award reasonable attorney's fees incurred by the debtor.

(6) *No action under this section may be brought more than six years after the violations occurred.*

. . .

§6.109. Assurance of discontinuance

If it is claimed that a person has engaged in conduct *which could be* subject to an order by the administrator, section 6.108, or by a court, sections 6.110 to 6.112, the administrator may accept an assurance in writing that the person will not engage in the same or in similar conduct in the future. *Such an assurance may include any, or any combination, of the following: stipulations for the voluntary payment by the creditor of the costs of investigation or of an amount to be held in escrow as restitution to debtors aggrieved by past or future conduct of the creditor or to cover costs of future investigation, or admissions of past specific acts by the creditor or that such acts violated this Act or other statutes. A violation of an assurance of discontinuance shall be a violation of this Act.*

§6.110. Injunctions against violations of act

The administrator shall bring a civil action to restrain any person from violating this Act.

*In such an action the court may make such orders or judgments as may be necessary to prevent the use or employment by a person of any practices prohibited by this Act, to reform contracts to conform to this Act or to rescind contracts in which a violation has tended to induce the debtor to contract with the creditor, even though the debtors are not parties to the action. In such an action the administrator may also recover his reasonable costs of investigation and reasonable attorneys' fees incurred in bringing the action. An action under this section and an action under section 6.113 (1) may be brought jointly using a single complaint.*

§6.113. Civil actions by administrator

(1) After demand, the administrator may bring a civil action against a creditor for *any violation listed in section 5.202.* An action may relate to transactions with more than one debtor. If it is found that *the creditor has made a violation so listed,* the court shall order the respondent to grant to the debtor or debtors *the remedies established in section 5.202, subsection (1) or (2), whichever is appropriate.* Refunds and penalties to which the debtor is entitled pursuant to this subsection may be set off against the debtor's obligation. If a debtor brings an action against a creditor to recover an excess charge or civil penalty, an action by the administrator to recover for the same excess charge or civil penalty shall be stayed while the debtor's action is pending and shall be dismissed if the debtor's action is dismissed with prejudice or results in a final judgment granting or denying the debtor's claim.

(2) The administrator may bring a civil action against a creditor or a person acting in his behalf to recover a civil penalty for willfully violating this Act, and if the court finds that the defendant has engaged in repeated *violations or a* willful violation of this Act, it may assess a civil penalty of no more than $5,000.

# ANOTHER "ASSAULT UPON THE CITADEL": LIMITING THE USE OF NEGOTIABLE NOTES AND WAIVER-OF-DEFENSE CLAUSES IN CONSUMER SALES

EDWARD J. MURPHY*

## I. INTRODUCTION

"The assault upon the citadel of privity is proceeding in these days apace."[1] It is doubtful that the master stylist, Justice Cardozo, could have foreseen how adaptable his metaphor would prove to be. Dean Prosser, himself a stylist of note, used it in his classic descriptions of the "fall" of the privity of contract defense in products liability cases.[2] It is he who is primarily responsible for burning the dictum into the memory of a generation of lawyers.[3] Can others of us who use it be blamed for recognizing a good thing when we see it?

Another "assault" which is going forward in the consumer sales area has as its objective ("citadel") the use of negotiable notes or waiver-of-defense clauses in contracts, whereby Transferee of Dealer may successfully proceed against Buyer despite the existence of a defense (such as failure of consideration or breach of warranty) which the latter could interpose if sued by Dealer. The ornithological breakdown of the combatants, who on occasion will remark that this is "a different kind of war," is roughly as follows: the "hawks" come mainly from the ranks of the academic community and the executive branch of the government. The "doves" are, for the most part, businessmen engaged in consumer credit activity. Judges and legislators can be found in both camps, and there are a wide variety of other species.

The militant "hawk" sees this war as part of the "larger struggle" for the protection of consumers ("victims of aggression"), and he presses for total abolition ("unconditional surrender"). He is, therefore, disinclined to negotiate a compromise, believing that such a negotiated settlement ("appeasement") would only encourage the

---

* Professor of Law, Notre Dame Law School.

1 Ultrameres Corp. v. Touche, 255 N.Y. 170, 180, 174 N.E. 441, 445 (1931).

2 Prosser, *The Assault Upon the Citadel (Strict Liability to the Consumer)*, 69 YALE L.J. 1099 (1960); Prosser, *The Fall of the Citadel (Strict Liability to the Consumer)*, 50 MINN. L. REV. 791 (1966).

3 A student who quoted the Cardozo dictum in his examination booklet appended this postscript: "I want you to know this is the first thing I have memorized since The Charge of the Light Brigade in the seventh grade."

enemy to greater, long-term effort. He favors escalation of the conflict and demands nothing short of military victory.

The extreme "dove," on the other hand, believes the war to be totally misconceived and misdirected. ("The wrong war, in the wrong place, at the wrong time.") He sees it as but another attempt by the "establishment" ("the industrial-military complex") to impinge upon the freedom of market participants to handle their own affairs. He questions whether there can be such a thing as a real military victory and insists the war effort is diverting resources from "domestic" programs, such as consumer "education." In short, he favors "unilateral withdrawal."

The "citadel" in this instance appears to be firmly established in both law and practice. The emergence in our legal system of the concept of negotiability has been of inestimable value in facilitating commercial transactions. It is an important part of "the triumph of the good faith purchaser," aptly characterized as "one of the most dramatic episodes in our legal history."[4] A high-energy economic system is dependent upon the free flow of commerce; accordingly, impediments to voluntary commercial exchange should be kept to a minimum.[5] If the purchaser of a right evidenced by a negotiable note can prevail despite the availability of "personal defenses" of the maker, the inducement to purchase will be intensified. Increasing the purchaser's risk, as by refusing to provide insulation against such defenses of the maker, would, inexorably, tend to depress purchases. This all builds toward the implementation of a basic policy or presupposition of our commercial law structure: that a high volume of economic exchange is a prime social desideratum.[6] Similarly, the freedom of contracting parties to insert in the agreement a clause whereby one of them waives certain defenses as against the other's transferee will likely have the salutary effect of expediting transactions. Indeed, the insertion of a waiver clause is an attempt to achieve "negotiability by contract"; *i.e.*, an attempt to invest the contract

---

4 Gilmore, *The Commercial Doctrine of Good Faith Purchase*, 63 YALE L.J. 1057 (1954).

5 *See generally* I. PATERSON, THE GOD OF THE MACHINE (1964), for a fascinating study of the political, economic and social conditions believed to be conducive to a dynamic economy.

6 "I do not think there is any single fact more important for men to recognize, with all its implications, than this single one—*that their individual well-being, as well as that of the whole society, is determined by the volume of exchanges going on in the whole society.*" H. SCHERMAN, THE PROMISES MEN LIVE BY 393 (1938) (italics in original).

with negotiable qualities without compliance with the usual statutory formalities of negotiable instruments. There is here, also, the added fact that our tradition has been one of maximizing the power of parties to establish, by agreement, the obligations they wish to assume. This freedom of contract is but one manifestation of a basic freedom of thought and action endemic to our social system. Even as to that minority group called businessmen, we presume a permission to do whatever is not lawfully forbidden. The burden of justifying a limitation upon freedom of action, including freedom of contract, is upon the one who insists upon the restraint. Professor Havighurst put it well: "Just as there must be 'freedom for the thought that we hate,' so there must also be, in a measure, freedom for the contract that we hate."[7]

## II. "THE ASSAULT UPON THE CITADEL . . ."

The "assault" is mounted by an impressive coalition of forces, employing the most potent and sophisticated of weapons. The attack is coordinated with a massive effort being waged in the courts, the legislatures, the legal periodicals, the popular press, and elsewhere, under the banner of "consumer protection" or "consumer rights." Neither the general war nor the isolated battle is new to our time,[8] but the conflict is building to unprecedented intensity as new offensives are being unleashed.[9] There will, perforce, be little room

---

7 H. HAVIGHURST, THE NATURE OF PRIVATE CONTRACT 124-25 (1961).

8 *See* Friedman, *Law, Rules, and the Interpretation of Written Documents*, 59 Nw. U.L. REV. 751 (1965). Professor Friedman, in this thoughtful article, refers to historical examples of judicial and legislative erosion of the traditional doctrine protecting holders in due course of negotiable instruments executed by consumers. He cites a 1901 Wisconsin statute which required "that any promissory note 'taken or given for any lightning rod, patent, patent right, stallion, or interest therein' must bear on its face 'in red ink' the words: 'The consideration for this note is the sale of a lightning rod, patent, patent right, stallion, or interest therein.' Notes subject to the statute were non-negotiable." He comments: "The seemingly strange Wisconsin list was actually a catalogue of some common ways in which certain smooth operators induced farmers to part with their hard-earned money." *Id.* at 758-59.

9 Potentially, the most significant is the draft of a Uniform Consumer Credit Code being prepared under the auspices of the National Conference of Commissioners on Uniform State Laws. This "U3C" will be a comprehensive regulatory statute touching many aspects of consumer credit, incidental features of which will be to limit substantially the use of waiver-of-defense clauses and negotiable instruments in consumer transactions. *See* Jordan and Warren, *A Proposed Uniform Code for Consumer Credit*, 8 B.C. IND. & COM. L. REV. 441 (1967). As an aside, a friend remarked that to be exposed to a U.C.C.C. after just becoming accustomed to the U.C.C. is apt to make one "C"-sick! [See note 1 to Prof. Spanogle's article, this issue.—ED.].

for neutral observers, and, to leave the metaphor, debate on all aspects of all questions becomes imperative.

Turning, first, to waiver-of-defense clauses, what are the objectives of those who would deny parties the freedom to agree, in a sales contract, that ordinary defenses available against the seller cannot be asserted against his transferee? Many arguments have been advanced in the legal periodical literature and the cases, ranging from an insistence that such clauses are *per se* objectionable as violative of public policy to a claim that the use of such clauses in certain types of transactions (notably, consumer sales) is unfair and the practice should be curtailed. For example, it has been said that such clauses are violative of public policy as attempts to confer negotiability upon writings without compliance with formalities prescribed by statute.[10] But while some insist that these clauses are inherently objectionable, most of the criticism is based upon their use in consumer sales where they are made part of standard form contracts which are often never read or understood by the purchaser.[11] This case for abolition draws heavily upon market experience which

---

[10] Equipment Acceptance Corp. v. Arwood Can Mfg. Co., 117 F.2d 442 (6th Cir. 1941); American Nat'l Bank v. A. G. Sommerville, Inc., 191 Cal. 364, 216 P. 376 (1923); Motor Contract Co. v. Van Der Volgen, 162 Wash. 449, 298 P. 705 (1931); Industrial Loan Co. v. Grisham, 115 S.W.2d 214 (Mo. Ct. App. 1938). *See also* Quality Finance Co. v. Hurley, 337 Mass. 150, 148 N.E.2d 385 (1958).

[11] Conditional sale contracts are invariably written by sellers and finance companies for sellers and finance companies. They are often printed in unconscionably small type and presented to the buyer as a mere formality to be gotten out of the way after the parties have come to terms on price. Sometimes they are not even identified as conditional sale contracts but are euphemistically labeled "Easy Payment Plan" or something of the sort. The seller is usually justified in believing either that the buyer will not read the contract at all or will not understand it if he does wade through it. Even were the buyer to read and comprehend the avalanche of legal consequences which would greet any default on his part, there is not much he can do about it, for if he wants to buy an automobile or an appliance of some sort . . . on the installment plan he must sign one conditional sale contract or another, and they are all pretty much alike. There is no indication that competition in the automobile or appliance businesses, however keen, has extended to the point where dealers attempt to attract buyers by offering them a more favorable contract. It is against this background that we must view the plight of [a buyer] who staggers into a contract which could make him liable to pay the full price of an air-conditioning unit to a finance company, with which he had not even directly dealt, even though the vendor sells him a defective article . . . .

Warren, *Tools of Chattel Security Transactions in Illinois*, 1956 ILL. LAW FORUM 531, 543.

strongly indicates a lack of awareness on the part of the consumer and consequent absence of meaningful negotiation regarding such clauses. This data leads to a re-examination of freedom of contract in this context. It is contended that these clauses are hardly ever the product of informed, voluntary choice; hence, their invalidation in no way diminishes genuine free choice. There are others, of course, who believe that freedom of contract is too highly touted anyway, being based, it is sometimes said, on a now discredited laissez-faire economics.[12] Increasingly, writers are placing this and other related questions within the larger frame of consumer protection as an avowed effort to secure "social justice" for the impoverished.[13] The abolition of the waiver clause is thus viewed as but one step, and perhaps a minor one, in an all-out program for the protection of "unorganized consumers."[14] The goal is sometimes stated in terms of equalizing the bargaining power of the participants,[15] the arguments here being reminiscent of the labor law debates of the 30's.

The related question of using negotiable promissory notes in consumer sales involves virtually the same policy considerations. Again, it is urged that the use should be prohibited outright. The most telling objection is that ordinarily the buyer is not aware of the legal effect of signing a negotiable note.[16] It is argued the average buyer does not, and cannot be expected to, realize that defenses which he has against the merchant might not be available in a suit by the holder. One judicial critic said: "The average citizen, and particularly the financially unimportant, [is] no more likely to know

---

12 *E.g.*, Shuchman, *Consumer Credit By Adhesion Contracts*, 35 TEMP. L.Q. 125 (1962).

13 *E.g.*, Willging, *Installment Credit: A Social Perspective*, 15 CATHOLIC. U.L. REV. 45 (1965).

14 *See* Comment, *Translating Sympathy for Deceived Consumers into Effective Programs for Protection*, 114 U. PA. L. REV. 395 (1966). Frequent reference is made in contemporary literature to the "unorganized" consumers. Perhaps President Kennedy set the style in his 1962 message to Congress concerning consumer programs: "Consumers, by definition, include us all. They are the largest economic group in the economy, affecting and affected by almost every public and private economic decision. Two-thirds of all spending in the economy is by consumers. But they are the only important group in the economy who are not effectively organized . . . ." 108 CONG. REC. 4167 (1962).

15 *E.g.*, Note, *New Consumer Credit Reforms in Illinois*, 17 DE PAUL L. REV. 194 (1967).

16 *See* Friedman, *supra* note 8. Professor Friedman, recalling the law merchant origins of negotiable instruments, reminds us that the rules of negotiable instruments were originally "class rules," binding only that group (merchants) who could be expected to know the legal effect of such instruments.

the law of negotiable paper . . . than the holding in Shelley's Case."[17] But even if, perchance, the buyer should know something of the law of negotiable paper (as, for example, that a failure of consideration defense cannot be successfully interposed in a suit by a holder in due course) it is nonetheless inappropriate to apply that law in the usual, garden-variety case. This argument relies heavily upon the history of negotiable instruments. Emphasis is placed upon the fact that it was the facilitation of negotiation that precipitated recognition of the negotiable note. It was desirable that these instruments be able to circulate freely; hence, impediments were discouraged. But, it is argued, in consumer cases it is rare that the instrument travels beyond the safe of the first transferee, the financial institution which purchases the paper from the merchant. Thus, the basic reason for insulating the holder from defenses the maker has against the payee vanishes. *Ergo . . . cessante ratione legis, cessat et ipsa lex.*[18]

Supporting reasons for denying holder in due course status to the purchaser of consumer paper are of a more pragmatic nature. To deprive the consumer of the right to withhold payment is to deprive him of the most potent weapon he has to enable him to receive that which he was promised. Although he does retain his right to proceed against the merchant after making payment to the financer, this, realistically, may be quite illusory. Apart from the burden of securing legal representation (the cost of which may be prohibitive in light of the amount involved), there is no assurance that a judgment against the merchant can be collected. By contrast, one could reasonably expect a financial institution both to investigate carefully the merchants from whom it buys paper and to arrange for reimbursement (through repurchase agreements, reserve accounts, buying the note with recourse, etc.) for losses sustained by reason of the merchants' defaults.[19] The added cost to the financer might ultimately result, because of higher discount rates, in increased costs to consumers, but this, on balance, is still a more intelligent way to proceed. Better to have the financial institution bear this cost initially; it is usually in a better position to absorb the cost and can spread the

---

[17] Buffalo Indus. Bank v. De Marzio, 162 Misc. 742, 743, 296 N.Y.S. 783, 785 (Buffalo City Ct. 1937).

[18] The reason for the law ceasing, the law itself ceases. *See* Jones, *Finance Companies as Holders in Due Course of Consumer Paper,* 1958 WASH. U.L.Q. 177. Professor Jones calls this the problem of ". . . the negotiable instrument which is never negotiated." *Id.* at 191.

[19] *See* Note, *Consumer Sales Financing: Placing the Risk for Defective Goods,* 102 U. PA. L. REV. 782, 791-93 (1954).

risk over the entire business. Finally, it is contended that the experience in states where the financer does not obtain holder in due course status does not indicate that the consequences are such as to either curtail the purchase of consumer paper or significantly increase the costs.[20]

## III.  " . . . Is Proceeding In These Days Apace."

How have the foregoing arguments, or variants thereof, fared in the courts and in the legislative assemblies? There is, first of all, a trend in the cases favoring some circumscription of holder in due course status for financial institutions purchasing consumer paper from merchants.[21] Likewise, there is legislation of comparatively

---

20 Felsenfeld, *Some Ruminations About Remedies in Consumer-Credit Transactions,* 8 B.C. IND. & COM. L. REV. 535, 551-52 (1967); Sutherland, *Article 3—Logic, Experience and Negotiable Paper,* 1952 WIS. L. REV. 230, 239-40; Vernon, *Priorities, the Uniform Commercial Code and Consumer Financing,* 4 B.C. IND. & COM. L. REV. 531, 547 (1963).

It has been suggested that from both the buyer's and financing agency's point of view, the issues of negotiability and waiver of defense have been greatly exaggerated in importance. It is said that the financing agency, prior to asserting its rights against the buyer, will attempt to settle honest claims by having the dealer make appropriate adjustments, thereby preserving the latter's reputation in the community. Failing this, resort will be had to the dealer's reserve account or his recourse indorsement. Only in cases where the dealer is insolvent, or where the financing agency and he are united in interest, will the buyer be called upon to make good his promise even though the seller has not performed his part of the bargain. Thus, it is argued, only in an infinitesimal number of retail installment sale transactions is the buyer harmed by his agreement to waive his defenses or by having given a negotiable instrument.

Conceding that no protection is needed in the vast majority of cases, protection in the remaining ones must come from the legislature, for it is also agreed that the buyer is unable to provide it for himself. Moreover, to say that the problem is not substantial is to look only to the reported decisions, few in number. It is to overlook the larger number of cases which either never reach an appellate level or never go to trial. The buyer who is being protected by retail installment legislation is normally one who cannot afford the luxury of a lawsuit and may, therefore, be forced as a practical matter to submit to the demands of the financing agency though he has an otherwise valid claim.

Project, *Legislative Regulation of Retail Installment Financing,* 7 U.C.L.A. L. REV. 618, 750 (1960).

21 For exhaustive annotation, see 44 A.L.R.2d 8 (1955) and supplemental material. *See also* Jones, *Finance Companies as Holders in Due Course of Consumer Paper,* 1958 WASH. U.L.Q. 176, for a comprehensive survey of judicial opinion dealing with this subject.

recent vintage withdrawing such status.[22] A concomitant trend, in both case law and legislation, can be discerned as regards waiver-of-defense clauses.[23] Indeed, the most striking development of all has been the emergence of important statutes prohibiting or limiting the use of waiver clauses in various types of consumer transactions.[24]

---

[22] Cal. Retail Installment Sales Act, CAL. CIV. CODE §§ 1803.2(a), 1810.9 (West Supp. 1967); Conn. Home Solicitation Sales Act, PUB. ACT 749 (West Conn. Leg. Ser. 1063, 1967); Del. Retail Installment Sales Law, DEL. CODE ANN. tit. 6, § 4342 (West Supp. 1966); Hawaii Retail Installment Sales Act, HAWAII REV. LAWS § 201A-17(d) (Supp. 1965); Ill. Consumer Fraud Act, ILL. ANN. STAT. ch. 121½, § 262D (Smith-Hurd Supp. 1967); Md. Retail Installment Sales Act, MD. ANN. CODE art. 83, § 147 (1957); Mich. Home Improvement Finance Act, MICH. COMP. LAWS § 445.1207 (1967); N.Y. Retail Installment Sales Act, N.Y. PERS. PROP. LAW § 403(1), (2) (McKinney, 1962); Pa. Home Improvement Finance Act, PA. STAT. ANN. tit. 73, § 500-207 (Supp. 1967); Pa. Motor Vehicle Sales Finance Act, PA. STAT. ANN. tit. 69, § 615(g) (1965); Pa. Goods and Services Installments Sales Act, PA. STAT. ANN. tit. 69, § 1302, 1909 (Supp. 1967); Vt. Consumer Fraud Act, VT. STAT. ANN. tit. 9, § 2455 (Supp. 1967); Wash. Credit Disclosure Act, WASH. REV. CODE ANN. § 63.14020 (Supp. 1967). *Cf.* Ill. Retail Installment Sales Act, ILL. ANN. STAT. ch. 121½ § 517 (Smith-Hurd Supp. 1967); Ill. Motor Vehicle Sales Act, ILL. ANN. STAT. ch. 121½, § 576 (Smith-Hurd Supp. 1967).

[23] *See* 44 A.L.R.2d 8, 92-96, 162-72 (1955) and supplemental material.

[24] Alaska Retail Installment Sales Act, ALASKA STAT. § 45.10.140 (1962); Cal. Automobile Sales Finance Act, CAL. CIV. CODE § 2983.5 (West Supp. 1967); Cal. Retail Installment Sales Act, CAL. CIV. CODE §§ 1804.1-.2 (West Supp. 1967); Conn. Home Solicitation Sales Act, PUB. ACT 749 (West Conn. Leg. Ser. 1063, 1967); Del. Retail Installment Sales Act, DEL. CODE ANN. tit. 6, § 4311-2 (West Supp. 1966); Hawaii Retail Installment Sales Act, HAWAII REV. LAWS § 201A-17(d) (Supp. 1965); Ill. Consumer Fraud Act, ILL. ANN. STAT. ch. 121½, § 262D (Smith-Hurd Supp. 1967; Mass. Retail Installment Sales and Services Act, MASS. ANN. LAWS ch. 255D, § 10 (1968); Mich. Home Improvement Finance Act, MICH. COMP. LAWS §§ 445.1206, 445.1208 (1967); Mich. Retail Installment Sales Act, MICH. COMP. LAWS §§ 445.864, -5 (1967); Miss. Motor Vehicle Sales Finance Act, MISS. CODE ANN. § 8075-13 (Supp. 1966); Nev. Retail Installment Sale of Goods and Services Act, NEV. REV. STAT. § 97.275 (1965); N. Mex. Retail Installment Sales Act, N.M. STAT. ANN. § 50-16-5 (Supp. 1967); N.Y. Retail Installment Sales Act, N.Y. PERS. PROP. LAW § 403(1), (2) (McKinney, 1962); N.Y. Motor Vehicle Retail Installment Sales Act, N.Y. PERS. PROP. LAW § 302 (McKinney Supp. 1967); Pa. Home Improvement Finance Act, PA. STAT. ANN. tit. 73, § 500-409 (Supp. 1967); Pa. Motor Vehicle Sales Finance Act, PA. STAT. ANN. tit. 69, § 615 (1965); Pa. Goods and Services Installment Sales Act, PA. STAT. ANN. tit. 69, §§ 1401, 1402 (1967); Tex. Retail Installment Sales Act, TEX. REV. CIV. STATS. ANN. art. 5069-6.07 (Vern. Supp. 1967); Tex. Motor Vehicle Installment Sales Act, TEX. REV. CIV. STATS. ANN. art. 5069-7.07, -8 (Vern. Supp. 1967); Vt. Consumer Fraud Act, VT. STAT. ANN. tit. 9, § 2455 (Supp. 1967); Wash. Credit Disclosure Act, WASH. REV. CODE ANN. § 63.14.020 (Supp. 1967). *Cf.* Ill. Retail Installment Sales Act, ILL. ANN. STAT. ch. 121½, § 517 (Smith-Hurd Supp. 1967); Ill. Motor Vehicle Retail Installment Sales Act, ILL. ANN. STAT. ch. 121½, § 576 (Smith-Hurd Supp. 1967).

## A. *Judicial Developments*

A 1967 decision of the Supreme Court of New Jersey, *Unico v. Owen*,[25] is illustrative of a developing judicial attitude. The case has the classic syndrome—(1) enticement by advertising (140 albums of stereophonic records for 698 dollars, plus a Motorola stereo record player "without separate charge"); (2) seller's agent contacting customer at home, with the resultant execution of a printed form "retail installment contract" or time payment plan and a negotiable promissory note; (3) fine print clauses in the contract, including an undertaking by the buyer "not to set up any claim against such seller as a defense, counterclaim or offset to any action by any assignee for the unpaid balance of the purchase price or for possession of the property"; (4) the immediate assignment of the contract and negotiation of the note to the plaintiff finance company (on forms supplied by the plaintiff and with the latter's name printed as assignee); (5) the subsequent realization by the buyer that written terms were not congruent with what he was led to believe on the basis of the advertisement; (6) the seller's subsequent insolvency and default in performance;[26] and (7) the plaintiff, as assignee of the contract and holder of the note suing for the balance due, claiming that failure of consideration is unavailing as a defense in view of (a) the waiver clause in the contract and (b) its status as holder in due course of the note.

The defendant won in the trial court, and the appellate division affirmed. The supreme court's affirmation was accompanied by an opinion of Justice Francis, speaking for a unanimous court. Justice

---

25 50 N.J. 101, 232 A.2d 405 (1967).

26 The lack of congruence between advertisement and contract was striking. Instead of a "free stereo" accompanying the purchase of 140 record albums for the price of 698 dollars, there was an agreement to pay 819.72 dollars over a three year period in monthly installments of 22.97 dollars. The 819.72 dollars included cash price of 698 dollars, "official fee" of 1.40 dollars (presumably cost of recording contract in County Register's Office) and "time price differential" or interest of 150.32 dollars, less 30 dollars down payment. More significantly, while the payments were to be made over a three-year period, the delivery of the albums, at the rate stipulated in the contract (12 at the inception, 12 at six month intervals) would take five years and four months! As the court remarked, "this means that 40% of the albums, although fully paid for, would still be in the hands of the seller." *Id.* at 107-08, 232 A.2d at 409.

The buyer received the stereo player and the original 12 albums, but despite his continuing to pay 12 monthly installments (total 303.24 dollars, including 30 dollars down payment) he never received another album. The deliveries ceased because of the seller's insolvency.

Francis, it will be recalled, was the author of the opinion in *Henningsen v. Bloomfield Motors.*[27] *Henningsen* proved to be a most potent weapon in the "assault upon the citadel of privity." It is quite possible that *Unico,* like *Henningsen,* will become a landmark. Neither opinion breaks new ground or offers a startlingly innovative approach, but each is a forthright, carefully documented exposition that comes along at a propitious moment.

The court was able to point to a significant and growing body of case precedent, where, in comparable situations, the plaintiff failed to qualify as a holder in due course.[28] In general, this refusal to insulate the holder from ordinary personal defenses of the maker (failure of consideration, breach of warranty, fraudulent misrepresentation, etc.) has been predicated upon the "close connection," "participation" or "involvement" of the holder in the transaction as indicative of a lack of good faith.[29]

This fascinating chapter of negotiable instruments law began with *Commercial Credit Co. v. Childs,*[30] a 1940 decision of the Arkansas Supreme Court. It was a typical transaction: Buyer executes a conditional sales contract and installment note; Dealer sells the paper to Finance Company. What was atypical was Buyer's ability to assert against Finance Company a defense based on Dealer's fraudulent misrepresentation. The defense was not one which could, by statute, be asserted against a holder in due course absent a showing of actual knowledge. The court explained its position as follows:

> We think appellant was so closely connected with the entire transaction or with the deal that it can not be heard to say that it, in good faith, was an innocent purchaser of the instrument for value before maturity. It financed the deal, prepared the instrument, and on the day it was executed took an assignment of it from [the dealer]. Even before it was executed it prepared the written assignment thereon to itself. Rather than being a purchaser of the instrument after its execution it was to all intents

27 32 N.J. 358, 161 A.2d 69 (1960).

28 The note was executed on November 6, 1962, after New Jersey had adopted the U.C.C. but before its effective date of January 1, 1963. Therefore, the requirements of due course holding were those specified in the Uniform Negotiable Instruments Act.

29 *See* note 21 *supra.*

30 199 Ark. 1073, 137 S.W.2d 260 (1940). Taylor v. Atlas Security Co., 213 Mo. App. 282, 249 S.W. 746 (1923), can be viewed as an antecedent of *Childs,* but the court in *Taylor* emphasized evidence from which actual knowledge of the dealer's fraud could be inferred. *See* Note, *Finance Company as a Holder in Due Course,* 28 NOTRE DAME LAWYER 251 (1953).

and purposes a party to the agreement and instrument from the beginning.[31]

The wedge had entered. Hereafter, counsel throughout the country would be citing *Childs.* The effort would prove futile in most cases, but there would be notable successes as well. Moreover, as time goes on the rationale for a *Childs*-like approach becomes more explicitly keyed to considerations of consumer protection. For example, in *Mutual Finance Co. v. Martin*,[32] an influential Florida case, the court remarked:

> It may be that our holding here will require some changes in business methods and will impose a greater burden on the finance companies. We think the buyer—Mr. & Mrs. General Public—should have some protection somewhere along the line. We believe the finance company is better able to bear the risk of the dealer's insolvency than the buyer and in a far better position to protect his interests against unscrupulous and insolvent dealers.[33]

The "close participation" doctrine thus emerged and developed within the context of consumer financing where the goods are purchased for personal, family or household purposes. This is not to say that the doctrine has not been implemented in non-consumer, commercial cases, or that the requisite participation or involvement might not there be sufficient to negate good faith on the part of the transferee.[34] But it is in the consumer area that the underlying rationale seems most persuasive and where the impact has been the greatest. For example, in *Unico v. Owen*, the New Jersey court, after stating that it was "concerned here with a problem of consumer goods financing,"[35] proceeded, after the fashion of *Henningsen*, to detail reasons for the special treatment of standardized financing contracts involving the consumer goods purchaser. The issue was posed as

> the basic problem in consumer goods sales and financing . . . of balancing the interest of the commercial community in unrestricted negotiability of commercial paper against the interest of installment buyers of such goods in the preservation of their normal remedy of withholding payment when, as in this case,

---

31 Commercial Credit Co. v. Childs, 199 Ark. 1073, 1077, 137 S.W.2d 260, 262 (1940).
32 63 So. 2d 649 (Fla. Sup. Ct. 1953).
33 *Id.* at 653.
34 *E.g.*, International Finance Corp. v. Rieger, 272 Minn. 192, 137 N.W.2d 172 (1965); Commercial Credit Corp. v. Orange County Machine Works, 34 Cal. 2d 766, 214 P.2d 819 (1950).
35 Unico v. Owen, 50 N.J. 101, 110, 232 A.2d 405, 410 (1967).

the seller fails to deliver as agreed, and thus the consideration for his obligation fails.[36]

A similar emphasis upon the consumer aspects of the transaction is discernible in the court's invalidation of the waiver-of-defense clause. It took cognizance of section 9-206(1) of the Uniform Commercial Code which provides that "[s]ubject to any statute or decition which establishes a different rule for buyers of *consumer goods*" (emphasis added), a waiver-of-defense clause is valid. "In this section of the Code," the court states, "the Legislature recognized the possibility of need for special treatment of waiver clauses in consumer goods contracts."[37] After referring also to section 2-302 of the Code pertaining to "unconscionable contracts," the court concludes: "We see in the enactment of these two sections of the Code an intention to leave in the hands of the courts the continued application of common law principles in deciding in consumer goods cases whether such waiver clauses as the one imposed on Owen in this case are so one-sided as to be contrary to public policy."[38]

## B. *Legislative Response*

The references in *Unico* to the Uniform Commercial Code are most interesting. For this whole debate began in earnest in the councils of the U.C.C. drafting committees, and it continues in the discussions of those presently putting together the Uniform Consumer Credit Code. It is against the background of this protracted conflict of opinion that one can perhaps best evaluate the legislative response to the use of negotiable notes and waiver clauses in consumer sales.

The original design of the Uniform Commercial Code, as it appeared in the May 1949 draft, included significant sections regulating consumer financing.[39] Among these was a provision subjecting the holder in due course of a consumer's note to the latter's contract defenses if rights were asserted against the collateral.[40] In an earlier version the Code also purported to make more difficult the attainment of due course status by adding to the ordinary subjective test of good faith ("honesty in fact") an objective standard (observance of "reasonable commercial standards").[41] Moreover, the draftsmen

---

36 *Id.* at 112, 232 A.2d at 411.
37 *Id.* at 125, 232 A.2d at 418.
38 *Id.*
39 UNIFORM COMMERCIAL CODE § 7-601 *et seq.* (May 1949 Draft).
40 *Id.* § 7-612.
41 UNIFORM COMMERCIAL CODE § 3-302 (1952 Official Text).

undertook to deal decisively with waiver clauses in consumer contracts. Section 9-206 of the 1952 Official Text provided as follows:

> An agreement by a buyer of consumer goods as part of the contract of sale that he will not assert against an assignee any claim or defense arising out of the sale is not enforceable by any person. If such a buyer as part of one transaction signs both a negotiable instrument and a security agreement even a holder in due course of the negotiable instrument is subject to such claims or defenses if he seeks to enforce the security interest either by proceeding under the security agreement or by attaching or levying upon the goods in an action upon the instrument.[42]

By these and related sections the Code authors took a firm stance in favor of regulating for the protection of consumer interests. But, due primarily to the exigencies of securing that consensus believed necessary for legislative success, they acceded to demands that these provisions be deleted or modified.[43] Those provisions in the original draft pertaining explicitly to consumer transactions were omitted from subsequent drafts. The standard of good faith for due course holding was modified to exclude the objective criteria introduced by the requirement of observance of "reasonable commercial standards."[44] And, most importantly, there was a basic restructuring of section 9-206 relative to waiver clauses, the effect of which was to positively encourage their use. Section 9-206(1) was amended to read as follows:

> Subject to any statute or decision which establishes a different rule for buyers of consumer goods, an agreement by a buyer that he will not assert against an assignee any claim or defense which he may have against the seller is enforceable by an assignee who takes his assignment for value, in good faith and without notice of a claim or defense, except as to defenses of a type which may be asserted against a holder in due course of a negotiable instrument under the Article on Commercial Paper (Article 3). A buyer who as part of one transaction signs both a negotiable instrument and a security agreement makes such an agreement.[45]

---

42 *Id.* § 9-206.

43 1 G. GILMORE, SECURITY INTERESTS IN PERSONAL PROPERTY 293-94 (1965); Kripke, *The Principles Underlying the Drafting of the Uniform Commercial Code*, 1962 ILL. LAW FORUM 321, 323; Skilton and Helstead, *Protection of the Installment Buyer of Goods Under the Uniform Commercial Code*, 65 MICH. L. REV. 1465, 1468 (1967).

44 UNIFORM COMMERCIAL CODE § 3-302 (1957 Official Text). For a critique, *see* Littlefield, *Good Faith Purchase of Consumer Paper: The Failure of the Subjective Test*, 39 S. CAL. L. REV. 48 (1966).

45 UNIFORM COMMERCIAL CODE § 9-206 (1957 Official Text).

It was in this form that the section was enacted throughout the country.[46] In sum, the more conspicuous regulatory elements were excised, and the overall thrust of the Code became decidedly one of facilitation rather than regulation.[47]

However, the effort for uniform regulation was resumed in 1964 as work began on the preparation of what will shortly be proposed for legislative adoption as the Uniform Consumer Credit Code.[48] This Code will regulate the whole spectrum of consumer credit, and it is understandable that consideration will again be given to the use of negotiable notes and waiver clauses in consumer transactions.

In the First Tentative Draft of the U3C, released in 1966, there were a number of proposed limitations upon creditors' remedies. One prohibited negotiable instruments in consumer credit sales altogether and another subjected a transferee to "all claims and defenses of the debtor against the seller arising out of the sale notwithstanding an agreement to the contrary."[49]

---

[46] All states except Louisiana have adopted the U.C.C.

[47] *See generally* Murphy, *Facilitation and Regulation in the Uniform Commercial Code*, 41 NOTRE DAME LAWYER 625 (1966).

[48] The U3C is a project of the National Conference of Commissioners of Uniform State Laws, a cosponsor of the U.C.C. The Special Committee charged with drafting responsibilities has, as of this writing (February, 1968), produced six "working drafts." The First Tentative Draft (Working Draft No. 1) was submitted to the National Conference as a Committee of the Whole at the 1966 annual meeting in Montreal. The Second Tentative Draft (Working Draft No. 4) was considered at the 1967 meeting in Hawaii. It is anticipated that a proposed final draft will be ready for promulgation by the National Conference at its annual meeting this August in Philadelphia. *See* Buerger, *Uniform Law Commissioners' Consumer Credit Project—4th Year*, 20 PERS. FIN. LAW Q. REV. 84 (1966); Dunham, *Second Draft of Proposed Uniform Consumer Credit Code Now Being Considered*, 21 PERS. FIN. LAW Q. REV. 75 (1967); Harper, *Proposed Uniform Consumer Credit Code Discussed at Annual Meeting of NCCUSL in Hawaii*, 21 PERS. FIN. LAW Q. REV. 119 (1967).

[49] Section 6.101 [Negotiable Instruments Prohibited.] In a consumer credit sale it is a violation of this Code for the seller to accept a negotiable instrument as evidence of the obligation of the debtor. If the face of the instrument bears the words "consumer note" the instrument is not negotiable. An instrument negotiable in form issued in violation of this section may be enforced as a negotiable instrument by a holder in due course according to its terms. The holder in due course is not subject to any of the liabilities set forth in section 6.201 and 7.204.

Section 6.102 [Transferee Subject to Defenses Against Seller]. Except as provided in section 6.101, with respect to a consumer credit sale a transferee of the seller's rights is subject to all claims and defenses of the debtor against the seller arising out of the sale notwithstanding an agreement to the contrary.

The draftsmen made their point unmistakable—negotiable notes and waiver-of-defense clauses have no place in consumer sales transactions. Of course, this thesis did not go unchallenged. The most controversy centered upon the treatment of waiver clauses, perhaps reflecting the fact that most sales financing today does not utilize a note, but relies upon a contract which includes a waiver clause.[50] This practice probably resulted in part from the encouragement of such clauses by section 9-206 of the Uniform Commercial Code, and also from a fear that because of the battering sustained in *Childs* and its progeny the holder in due course doctrine in consumer sales was rather shaky anyway. Hence, the fire was directed primarily against the provision subjecting a transferee to "all claims and defenses of the debtor against the seller arising out of the sale notwithstanding an agreement to the contrary." Some critics seized upon the reference to "claims" of the debtor. Would this mean, for example, that the transferee could be sued for the dealer's breach of warranty?[51]

By this time (1966) there were a number of state statutory provisions, found usually in Retail Installments Sales Acts, limiting the use of waiver clauses.[52] A few statutes prescribed outright abolition.[53] Others made validity dependent upon compliance with a notice requirement.[54] For example, under the New York statute the buyer was given ten days after receiving notice of the assignment within which to notify the assignee of "facts giving rise to the claim or defense" or otherwise lose the right to assert against the assignee any

---

[50] Based on interviews with Mr. Max A. Denney, Executive Vice President, American Industrial Bankers Association, and Mr. Paul R. Moo, South Bend attorney and member of the Advisory Committee of the U3C project.

[51] If so construed, this would open the possibility of recovery against the transferee of an amount in excess (perhaps far in excess) of the outstanding balance due from the buyer.

[52] *See generally* B. CURRAN, TRENDS IN CONSUMER CREDIT LEGISLATION (1965).

[53] Alaska (Retail Installments Sales Act, 1962); Massachusetts (Retail Installment Sales and Services Act, 1966); Mississippi (Motor Vehicle Sales Finance Act, 1958); Nevada (Retail Installment Sale of Goods and Services Act, 1965); New Mexico (Retail Installment Sales Act, 1965. For citations, see note 24 *supra*.

[54] California (Retail Installment Sales Act, 1959; Automobile Sales Finance Act, 1961); Delaware (Retail Installment Sales Act, 1960); Hawaii (Retail Installment Sales Act, 1963); Michigan (Retail Installment Sales Act, 1965; Home Improvement Finance Act, 1965); New York (Motor Vehicle Retail Installment Sales Act, 1956; Retail Installment Sales Act, 1957); Pennsylvania (Motor Vehicle Sales Finance Act, 1947; Home Improvement Finance Act, 1963; Goods and Services Installment Sales Act, 1966). For citations, *see* note 24 *supra*.

right of action or defense arising out of the sale which he might have against the seller.[55]

Other states had joined the ranks of these states or were in the process of doing so when the Second Tentative Draft of the Uniform Consumer Credit Code was released in 1967.[56] The negotiable note section, changed slightly, now reads as follows:

> Section 2.403. [Negotiable Promissory Notes Prohibited.] In a consumer credit sale or consumer lease the seller or lessor may not take a promissory note payable to order or to bearer as evidence of the obligation of the debtor. A promissory note payable to order or to bearer and otherwise negotiable in form issued in violation of this section may be enforced as a negotiable instrument by a holder in due course according to its terms. The holder in due course is not subject to any of the liabilities set forth in Section 5.201, 6.108(2) and 6.113(1).[57]

This section would seem to make virtually impossible the attainment of holder in due course status by the dealer's transferee. For the latter would in the ordinary situation know that the underlying transaction was a "consumer credit sale or consumer lease" and would be presumed to know that the law prohibits the seller from taking a negotiable note in such a transaction. This may not be true as regards a transferee farther down the line, and the statute seemingly recognizes the possibility of such a person qualifying and proceeding as a holder in due course.

The waiver provision was revised. Waiver clauses were outlawed, as before, and the transferee was subjected to "all claims and defenses of the debtor." But it was provided that "the transferee's liability . . . may not exceed the amount owing to the transferee at the time the claim or defense is asserted against the transferee." To further clarify this it was stated that the "[r]ights of the debtor under this section can only be asserted as a matter of defense to a claim by the transferee."[58] A proposal to offer, as an alternative, a provision pat-

---

[55] N.Y. PERS. PROP. LAW § 403(3) (1967).

[56] In 1967 statutes invalidating waiver clauses were passed in Connecticut (Home Solicitation Sales Act), Vermont (Consumer Fraud Act), and Washington (Credit Disclosure Act). Notice type provisions were enacted in Illinois (Consumer Fraud Act) and Texas (Motor Vehicle Installment Sales Act; Retail Installment Sales Act). Finally, two states shifted from notice type provisions to outright abolition: California (Retail Installment Sales Act) and Hawaii (Retail Installment Sales Act). For citations, see note 24 supra.

[57] UNIFORM CONSUMER CREDIT CODE § 2.403 (Second Tentative Draft, 1967).

[58] Id. § 2.404.

terned upon the New York statute (but with 45 instead of 10 days as the "cut-off period") was rejected.[59]

The Committee of the Whole, meeting in Hawaii in August, 1967, went over the draft, and there emerged from this meeting yet another revision of the waiver clause provision. It was a compromise. Instead of the single provision, alternatives were adopted. Alternative A, incorporating the notice requirement but with a substantially longer time period (six months), is as follows:

> Section 2.404. [Transferee Not Subject to Defenses Against Seller if Proper Notice of Transfer Given to Buyer.] (1) With respect to a consumer credit sale or lease, other than a sale or lease primarily for an agricultural purpose, an agreement by the buyer or lessee not to assert against a transferee a claim or defense arising out of the sale or lease is enforceable only by a transferee not related to the seller or lessor who acquires the buyer's or lessee's contract in good faith and for value, who gives the buyer or lessee notice of the transfer as provided in this section and who, within 6 months after the mailing of the notice of transfer, receives no written notice of the facts giving rise to the buyer's or lessee's claim or defense. The notice of transfer shall be in writing and addressed to the buyer or lessee at his address as stated in the contract, identify the contract, describe the goods or services, state the names of the seller or lessor and buyer or lessee, the name and address of the transferee, the amount payable by the buyer or lessee and the number, amounts and due dates of the instalments, and contain a conspicuous notice to the buyer or lessee that he has 6 months within which to notify the transferee in writing of any complaints, claims or defenses he may have against the seller or lessor and that if written notification of the complaints, claims or defenses is not given within the six-month period, the transferee will have the right to enforce the contract free of any claims or defenses the buyer or lessee may have against the seller or lessor.
>
> (2) A transferee does not acquire a buyer's or lessee's contract in good faith within the meaning of subsection (1) if the tranferee has knowledge or, from his course of dealing with the seller or lessor or his records, notice of substantial complaints by other buyers or lessees of the seller's or lessor's failure to perform his contracts with them and of the seller's or lessor's failure to remedy his defaults within a reasonable time after the transferee notifies him of the complaints.[60]

---

[59] *Id.* § 2.404, Comment.

[60] UNIFORM CONSUMER CREDIT CODE § 2.404 (Working Draft No. 6, 1967). Alternative A. A comment appended to the waiver clause provision of the First Tentative Draft referred to the notice type statutes as follows: "Several states, including New York and California, have provisions requiring the buyer to give notice within a stated

Alternative B, substantially the same as the provision in the Second Tentative Draft, reads as follows:

> Section 2.404. [Transferee Subject to Defenses.] With respect to a consumer credit sale or consumer lease, other than a sale or lease primarily for an agricultural purpose, a transferee of the rights of the seller or lessor is subject to all claims and defenses of the buyer or lessee against the seller or lessor arising out of the sale or lease notwithstanding an agreement to the contrary, but the transferee's liability under this section may not exceed the amount owing to the transferee at the time the claim or defense is asserted against the transferee. Rights of the buyer or lessee under this section can only be asserted as a matter of defense to or set-off against a claim by the transferee.[61]

The compromise of offering alternative formulations was preceded by a public hearing in June, 1967, in Chicago and by debate in the Committee of the Whole meeting in Hawaii later that summer. A culling of a few of the comments from these sessions may be suggestive of what can be expected on this issue as the U3C makes its way through legislative channels. The provision for abolition was hailed as "probably the most critically important to legal aid clients as far as the provisions of the Code are concerned."[62] Critics of the provision condemned it as the wrong approach which "completely undoes the [Uniform Commercial] Code."[63] It was defended as an attempt "to push the policing of the schlock merchant onto the private financial institutions, rather than let things roll along to the point where somebody decides to set up all sorts of regulatory commissions and regulatory bodies to punish the schlock merchant."[64] Another predicted it would "drive the small finance

---

period (commonly 10 or 15 days) to a transferee of defenses against the seller in order to preserve these defenses against the transferee. Experience has shown that a period of 10 or 15 days may be too short and that *a period of at least 30 days may be desirable*." UNIFORM CONSUMER CREDIT CODE § 6.102, Comment (First Tentative Draft). (emphasis added). The compromise incorporated in Working Draft No. 6 not only adopted a "cut-off period" of six months, it also added, in subsection 2, an elaboration of "good faith" which would make more difficult the transferee's acquiring insulation against "claims and defenses" the buyer has against the seller. Finally, there is no provision in Alternative A, as in Alternative B, limiting the buyer to asserting his rights as a matter of defense or to set-off against a claim by the transferee.

61 *Id.* § 2.404, Alternative B.

62 Proceedings, Public Hearing on Second Tentative Draft of the Uniform Consumer Credit Code 212 (June 16-17, 1967).

63 Proceedings, Committee of the Whole, Uniform Consumer Credit Code 195 (August 1-3, 1967).

64 *Id.* at 196.

companies out of business,"[65] with the consequence that "people who need financing most are going to be least likely to get it. . . ."[66] Turning to the six month time period of Alternative A, some thought the time too long ("I'm surprised to hear anything as long as six months suggested."[67]), others thought there ought to be no time limit at all, and still others believed the six month period to be about right ("I feel that the alternative gives the buyer here a pretty fair protection."[68]). Near the end of the debate on this section, one man who thought the six month period too long ("If you can't find out what the hell's wrong with the outfit in less than six months, you are not very bright . . ."[69]) facetiously suggested: "Let's make it 123 days. That would be a unique provision."[70] The transcriber duly noted the "laughter" which followed, and the Chairman proceeded to call for a vote of the Committee. The compromise carried 26 to 18,[71] and thus the matter stands until the next round.

## IV. Conclusion

This movement to limit the use of negotiable notes and waiver-of-defense clauses is indeed "proceeding in these days apace." As noted, the judicial trend has been steady, if unspectacular. The legislative response, on the other hand, has been both steady and spectacular. New statutory provisions have appeared; old ones have been strengthened.[72] One can reasonably expect this general legislative trend to continue. Finally, there is, waiting in the wings, the Uniform Consumer Credit Code, which, when finally approved and submitted for legislative adoption, will contain provisions substantially limiting, if not preventing completely, the use of negotiable notes and waiver clauses in consumer transactions.

It is not a sufficient answer to say that the abolition of the waiver clause limits freedom of contract. For in most cases these clauses are found in standard form contracts which are not read or

---

65 Proceedings, Public Hearing on Second Tentative Draft of the Uniform Consumer Credit Code 217. (June 16-17, 1967).

66 *Id.*

67 Proceedings, Committee of the Whole, Uniform Consumer Credit Code 212 (August 1-3, 1967).

68 *Id.* at 210.

69 *Id.* at 216-17.

70 *Id.* at 217.

71 *Id.* at 217-18.

72 Especially significant in this respect was the abandonment in two States of a notice type waiver clause provision and the substitution of outright abolition. *See* authorities cited, note 56 *supra*.

understood by the consumer purchaser. While it may be affirmed as a general proposition that there should be a goal of maximizing the freedom of contracting parties to set the terms of their agreement, and I do so affirm, just what is their agreement or contract in the prototype transaction? This whole relationship of freedom of contract and the standard form, adhesion-type contract, has long been a matter of major concern. Actually, the basic question here is not so much what contracting parties should be free to do, but whether public authority should make available legal devices which afford transferees extraordinary advantage. This is obvious in the case of the negotiable instrument, the law from the beginning insisting upon certain special requirements as to both form and method of negotiation. But it is no less apparent as regards utilization of waiver-of-defense clauses, wherein there is the achievement of a kind of "negotiability by contract." Thus viewed, the issue is whether there is sufficient reason to permit the transferee to assert a right superior to that of his transferor. One important reason for supporting such a view is that such permission would help to facilitate commercial transactions. It would encourage the free flow of commerce, with the consequence of lower credit costs for the consuming public.

This need not, and in my opinion, should not be posed as an either-or question. For even if legislatures can be persuaded to invalidate these waiver clauses, for example, might not the accomplishment prove to be illusory? If lending institutions find the risks in the purchase of consumer sales paper to be unacceptable, what will prevent a shift to a pattern of direct lending, perhaps utilizing innovative procedures yet to be devised? To be sure, in implementing such a shift there would be problems, legal and otherwise, but it is surely an underestimation of business acumen and initiative to believe the task to be impossible. Recently a very knowledgeable observer reminded us of how the problem can shift almost as soon as the solution is adopted, leaving a residue of "statutory obsolescence."[73] Moreover, in terms of the interest in securing uniform legislation on the point, there is no assurance that state legislatures can be persuaded to outlaw waiver clauses completely. There is no consensus favoring such action within the ranks of the U3C drafting committees, and this presages difficulties in securing uniform legislative acceptance.

Alternatives to all-out support or rejection should be considered, not merely because of a desire to enhance the likeihood of wide-

---

[73] Gilmore, *On Statutory Obsolescence*, 39 U. Colo. L. Rev. 461 (1967).

spread legislative success, but in an effort to provide the best method of operation. A tested method is the type proposed as a U3C alternative, the making of waiver-of-defense clauses subject to compliance with a notice requirement which gives the buyer a certain number of days to lodge complaints and thereby preserve defenses. Prescinding, for the moment, from the "numbers game" (whether the cut-off period should be 10 days as in New York, 45 days as in a Pennsylvania statute, six months as in the U3C alternative, etc.), the basic approach has evident merit.[74] It does not give carte blanche to the transferee, nor does it make impossible the attainment of insulation against buyer's defenses. Hopefully, it is possible to strike a balance which will not significantly decrease the purchasing of consumer sales paper or increase the costs thereof, while at the same time affording the consumer reasonable protection.

How long should the cut-off period, the statute of limitations as some have dubbed it, be? The danger here is that the figure will be picked arbitrarily, or by hunch, rather than being based on relevant supporting data. If this is not to occur, and if the spectacle of having the compromise figure reflect no more than tactical give and take between competing interests is to be avoided, more information will have to be supplied. What kind of information? Basically, cost data, both in terms of increased costs to the financers and the losses sustained by consumers in being forced to pay without adequate recourse against the dealer. What has been the effect upon the cost of credit in those states where the use of waiver clauses or negotiable notes has been circumscribed by statute? Does the consumer have to pay more for credit? Does he have a more difficult time obtaining credit? Has there been a squeeze-out of the small financer? Additionally, would it not be helpful, especially in setting a cut-off period for waiver clauses, to have trustworthy data as to when dealer defaults and product defects ordinarily appear? To be sure, such information would produce no more than a general pattern, but it would be something to go on, certainly preferable to the apparent

---

74 "Claims of defective performance are thus available to the buyer for the limited period, but the statute also protects the assignee from fictitious defenses fabricated when the buyer discovers he is unable to pay the debt. Where there are latent defects in the goods, the risk of suing the seller is thrown upon the buyer, but considerations of the relative innocence of both parties and the desirability of a free flow of this kind of paper makes the provision seem meritorious." Hogan, *A Survey of State Retail Instalment Sales Legislation*, 44 CORNELL L.Q. 38, 67 (1958).

blank that appears now in the published materials. If industry representatives believe the six-month period of the U3C alternative to be unreasonably long, they would be well-advised to buttress their arguments with supporting data of this type.

Anything less than total and complete invalidation of waiver-of-defense clauses in consumer sales contracts will be viewed by many as inconsistent with a commitment to "consumer protection." I would submit that our commitment should not be to securing "protection" for the consumer, but "justice." The consumer is not entitled to "protection"; he is, the same as everyone else, entitled to his due. A waiver provision incorporating a reasonable cut-off period would not be demonstrably unjust and would provide a feasible solution.

# CONSUMER PROTECTION UNDER ARTICLE 2 OF THE UNIFORM COMMERCIAL CODE

Morris G. Shanker and Mark R. Abel*

Consumer protection from defective goods or unfair contracts has become a subject of increased attention with the establishment of legal assistance for indigent claimants who have been the victims of unscrupulous merchants. Lawyers are searching the Uniform Commercial Code for legal remedies for consumer wrongs. This article attempts to dissect the portion of the Uniform Commercial Code dealing with sales transactions, article 2, and chart some of the established and potential remedies available to the customer. There are two classes of cases in which consumer protection is most often needed. One involves transactions in which the buyer does not receive the quality of merchandise for which he had bargained. This class gives rise to claims dealing with warranties that may have attached during the sale. The second involves transactions in which the buyer receives merchandise in conformity to his expectations but other aspects of the agreement seem unfair. The latter class may give rise to arguments based on unconscionability or lack of good faith.

## I. Creation of Warranties

Where the goods are defective, the buyer's legal remedy will most often be an action for breach of warranty. Under the Code, there are two types of warranties relating to the quality of the goods: express[1] and implied.[2] Each of these warranties contains subparts to give protection for different aspects of the sales transaction. The express warranty results from some affirmative act by the seller in attempting to promote his product. This action by the seller may take the form of a promise or an affirmation with respect to the

---

* This article was prepared by members of the Editorial Board under the direction of Mr. Abel. It is an expansion and elaboration of an address given by Professor Shanker, Professor of Law, Case Western Reserve University, at a seminar on law and poverty in Columbus, Ohio in 1967, first published in Ohio St. Legal Services Assoc., The Course on Law and Poverty: The Consumer (1967). Professor Shanker's co-operation in permitting the free use of his manuscript is gratefully acknowledged. However, the Editorial Board assumes full responsibility for the style and substance of this article. Ed.

1 Uniform Commercial Code § 2-313 [hereinafter cited as U.C.C.].

2 Id. §§ 2-314 (implied warranty of merchantability), 2-315 (implied warranty of fitness for particular purpose).

quality of his products. Most often this warranty will be created by an oral or written guarantee, but the word "guarantee" need not be present; in fact, many oral statements by the seller will be adequate to create this type of express warranty.[3] A less obvious express warranty is that the kind of goods sold will actually be delivered to the buyer. For example, if a seller promises to sell a heavy duty motor, he warrants both that a motor will be delivered to the buyer and that such motor will be a heavy duty one. It would seem that every sale agreement contains an express warranty, at least to the extent the description of the product carries a promise that the goods will be delivered and will conform to that description.[4] Express warranties are not limited to verbal promises of the seller but include use of a model or sample by a seller to indicate his goods to the buyer.[5]

Not all acts of the seller give rise to express warranties. There must also be shown some degree of reliance on the part of the buyer to transform an act of the seller into a warranty upon which an action for damages may be based. To create an express warranty under the Code the promise, affirmation, description, or sample must be part of the "basis of the bargain."[6] The basis of the bargain test is a change from the warranty test of the Uniform Sales Act which required that the affirmation or promise be "relied upon" by the buyer before a warranty would arise.[7] The Code, however, recognizes the reliance doctrine as being peculiar to estoppel, based on a subjective theory of contract and difficult of proof. It therefor creates a presumption that reliance has occurred by putting the seller to his proof that his statements could not have become the basis of the bargain. A broader and more objective standard is the result.

The second type of warranty which the Code recognizes is the

---

[3] *Id.* § 2-313(2). Puffing, as defined by this section, is excluded from the express warranty, since it cannot fairly be viewed as entering into the bargain. The presumption is created that any statements made by the seller become part of the basis of the bargain, and good reason to the contrary must be shown to exclude such statements from the express warranty. *See* § 2-313, Comment 3. *See also* Green Chevrolet Co. v. Kemp, 241 Ark. 62, 406 S.W.2d 142 (1966).

[4] *See* Smith v. Zimbalist, 2 Cal. App. 2d 324, 38 P.2d 170 (1934) for a pre-Code analysis of conformity to descripton.

[5] U.C.C. § 2-313(1)(c).

[6] *Id.* § 2-313.

[7] UNIFORM SALES ACT § 12, [hereinafter cited as SALES ACT]. Reliance was unnecessary in warranties of description and sample because both were implied warranties; SALES ACT §§ 14, 16.

implied warranty. One of these is the implied warranty of merchantability.[8] This warranty arises whenever a merchant[9] makes a sale of an item from his regular inventory, including food or drink wherever consumed. The other implied warranty recognized by the Code is the warranty of fitness for a particular purpose.[10] This warranty is implied where the buyer relies on the skill and judgment of the seller to furnish goods suitable for the buyer's particular purpose and the seller knows of this reliance.

Although the warranty terminology is similar to that used under the Sales Act,[11] a careful look at the sales warranties found in the Code will show that they are not precisely the same. The Code has done three important things to warranty law. First it enlarged warranty protection over that provided by the Sales Act. Thus warranties under the Code will arise more often and be broader in scope than the comparable warranties under the Sales Act. Abolition of the inducement-reliance requirement of express warranty will expand consumer recourse against the unscrupulous merchant. Inclusion of food and drink in the warranty of merchantability alters the rule in some jurisdictions.[12] The expansion of products liability through the warranty of merchantability is encouraged in section 2-314(3). Another change is the Code's clarification of the implied warranty of merchantability, the warranty lawyers rely upon most heavily in personal injury cases. In the Sales Act merchantability was undefined, and various interpretations of its content arose.[13] The Code sets forth six distinct requirements to meet the warranty,[14] while leaving room for judicial expansion. Third, the Code makes warranties cumulative.[15] The latter improvement eliminates the need to elect between warranties and permits claims to be made under any combination

---

8 U.C.C. § 2-314.

9 *Id.* § 2-104(1).

10 *Id.* § 2-315.

11 SALES ACT §§ 12-16.

12 This provision resolves a conflict among jurisdictions begun in the classic cases of Friend v. Childs Dining Hall Co., 231 Mass. 65, 120 N.E. 407 (1918) and Valeri v. Pullman Co., 218 F. 519 (S.D.N.Y. 1914). Ohio has long allowed recovery for injury by defective food or drink. *See* Yochem v. Gloria, Inc., 134 Ohio St. 427, 17 N.E.2d 731 (1938); Tipple v. High Street Hotel Co., 70 Ohio App. 397, 41 N.E.2d 897 (1941).

13 *See* Prosser, *The Implied Warranty of Merchantable Quality*, 27 MINN. L. REV. 117, 125-139 (1943).

14 U.C.C. § 2-314(2).

15 *Id.* § 2-317.

of the warranties, unless a particular combination would be unreasonable or inconsistent. Rules are provided for ascertaining the intention of the parties in the event cumulation is not possible.[16]

## II. PAROL EVIDENCE RULE

There may be a practical limit on a remedy based on warranty due to the parol evidence rule, which traditionally insured that when a contract had been reduced to writing the written terms would not be later contradicted by extrinsic or parol evidence. The parol evidence rule was firmly entrenched in our common law and is retained under the Code: "Terms . . . which are . . . set forth in a writing intended by the parties as a final expression of their agreement . . . may not be contradicted by evidence of any prior agreement or of a contemporaneous oral agreement. . . .[17]

The force of the rule was demonstrated in a recent Arkansas case, *Green Chevrolet Co. v. Kemp.*[18] In this case an automobile salesman had assured the buyer during oral negotiations that preceded the sale that the car was absolutely guaranteed for one year, and it was shown that such guarantee formed the basis of the bargain. But the written sales agreement said nothing about warranties. In fact, it stated that the consumer had fully examined the car, tested it and found it to be in first-class condition. The Arkansas Supreme Court said that evidence of the oral one year guarantee was not admissible. The written contract stating that the car was in first-class condition bound the parties and could not be contradicted by oral evidence. Fortunately there are some real limitations on the impact of the parol evidence rule, but lawyers often overlook them because they either do not understand the Code provisions, or they fail to analyze the Code or facts with imaginative minds.

### A. *Written Exclusions of Implied Warranties*

Under the Code, a written contractual term purporting to prevent any warranties from arising during a sale does not necessarily foreclose their existence. For example, section 2-316 requires that any written disclaimer of the implied warranty of merchantability must mention the word "merchantability." Furthermore, the

---

16 *Id.* These rules prefer specificity over inconsistent general language and express over implied warranties. Note, also, that the seller is estopped to assert the inconsistency where he has led the buyer to believe all warranties can be performed. U.C.C. 2-317, Comment 2.

17 *Id.* § 2-202.

18 241 Ark. 62, 406 S.W.2d 142 (1966).

disclaiming language must be conspicuous; the Sales Act approach permitting all warranties to be excluded by small print on the back of the written contract was abandoned by the Code. The new Code requirements are illustrated in a case recently decided by the Massachusetts Supreme Court. In *Hunt v. Perkins Machinery Co.,*[19] the disclaimers were on the back of the sales order and there was no signal on the front of the sales order, where the parties had signed, indicating further sales conditions were to be found on the back. The buyer therefore would become aware of the disclaimers found on the back only after he had already signed the contract on the front. The court held the disclaimers were ineffective because they were not conspicuous, and the buyer was allowed to sue on the implied warranties. The Code follows a similar approach in dealing with the implied warranty of fitness for purpose. To exclude this warranty, the exclusion must be in writing and must be conspicuous.[20]

## B. *Exclusion of Express Warranties*

Although implied warranties can be excluded by a written instrument if certain conditions are met, an express warranty found in the written agreement cannot be excluded. The express warranty arises because the seller has done something affirmative to push the sale. By reducing to writing a promise, affirmation, guarantee, or description, the seller has made an express warranty which he cannot escape by some language in the sales agreement seeking to negate or disclaim warranties. For example, if the sales agreement guarantees tires to run for 50,000 miles, two express warranties have arisen. One is that the goods delivered to the buyer will, in fact, be tires; the other is that the tires will run for 50,000 miles. Having made these two express warranties, the seller cannot in a later paragraph of the sales agreement say that there are no express warranties involved in the sale.[21]

## C. *Requirement of Finality*

Another important restriction on the scope of the Code's parol evidence rule is that it applies only where the writing is "intended by the parties as the final expression of their agreement."[22] Every

---

19 352 Mass. 535, 226 N.E.2d 228 (1967).

20 U.C.C. § 2-316(2).

21 *Id.* § 2-316(1).

22 *Id.* § 2-202.

writing connected with the sales transaction does not necessarily present parol evidence problems. Writings containing disclaimers of warranties, which are delivered to the buyer after the transaction is closed, can hardly be classified as a writing intended by both parties as the final expression of their agreement. It is nothing more than a writing prepared by the seller for his own self-serving purposes and does not give the seller the right to claim the protection of the parol evidence rule. In a recent California case the court stated that:

> Attempts to escape liability for warranties . . . by disclaimers made *"upon* or *after* delivery of the goods, by means of language on an invoice, receipt or similar notice," are ineffectual "unless the buyer assents or he is charged with knowledge of non warranty as to the transactions."[23]

The writing must be shown to be one which both parties have agreed shall be their expression of the contract before the parol evidence rule will be applicable.

### D. *Consistent Additional Terms*

When the parties have agreed to express their sales contract in a writing, section 2-202 makes it clear that the writing is binding only as to statements actually contained in the writing. If there are aspects of the agreement not contained in the writing, these additional matters may be established by extrinsic evidence. The only restriction on the introduction of additional terms is that these terms must be consistent with the writing. For example, the parties may have signed a sales agreement which contained the price, the delivery date and the credit terms. However, if the written agreement is silent as to warranties the writing will be binding only on the matters of the price, delivery and credit terms, and extrinsic evidence may be introduced to show warranties which are not covered by the writing and do not contradict the terms of the writing.

### E. *Explanation of Language*

The parol evidence rule does not prevent a party from using extrinsic evidence to explain what the language in the writing was intended to mean. This is true even though the language on its face may appear to be unambiguous. Under the Code, the plain meaning of the language found in a sales agreement may not be con-

---

[23] Klein v. Asgrow Seed Co., 246 Cal. App. 2d 87, 102, 54 Cal. Rptr. 609, 616 (1966).

trolling.[24] The Code is more interested in what meaning the parties actually intended to attach to the particular language.[25] Evidence of their intended meaning may be found in their past dealings and by the usages of the trade. Thus, the Code permits extrinsic evidence to be introduced to show that the word "dozen" when used by bakers in a sales contract really means thirteen. Likewise, a thousand sacks of sugar in the sugar industry may not mean one thousand at all. Instead, it may mean a thousand sacks plus or minus ten per cent. Although no cases have been found where this type of evidence was introduced to clarify a warranty, the legal principle would certainly apply to warranty language. For example, the words "three months warranty" in a particular industry, or between a particular seller and a particular buyer, may really mean four months of free service. If it can be demonstrated that sellers in that trade, as a matter of course, normally give service beyond the precise warranty period, the customer may get the benefit of the extended warranty protection.

## F.  *Future Agreements*

Another important limitation on the parol evidence rule is that the rule only prevents introduction of extrinsic evidence of understandings that the parties agreed upon prior to or contemporaneously with the execution of the writing.[26] Thus evidence of a one year guarantee given after the parties signed a contract containing only a six month warranty would not be excluded by the rule. In the context of consumer sales transactions one finds that sellers will often make statements about the quality of their goods after purchaser has signed a written contract purporting to exclude warranties. At first it might appear that subsequent statements would always fail to meet the "basis of the bargain" requirement for express warranties.[27] But subsequent agreements become modifications of the original contract and need no new consideration to be binding on the parties.[28] The only exception to this rule is where the parties agreed in the written contract that no oral modification of the original agreement would be permitted.[29] Even with such a provision subsequent oral modification might be effective as a waiver,[30]

---

24 U.C.C. § 2-202 and Comment 3.
25 *Id.*
26 *Id.* § 2-202.
27 *See* note 7 *supra* and accompanying text.
28 U.C.C. § 2-209(1).
29 *Id.* § 2-209(2).
30 *Id.* § 2-209(5).

or the buyer may not have separately signed the term barring future oral modification in the original contract, as required by the Code to make such a prohibition effective.[31]

## G. Fraud and Mistake

Another method of circumventing the parol evidence restriction is to demonstrate that the agreement has been tainted with fraud. Historically, attempts to prove fraud were not barred by the parol evidence rule because the policy favoring a just result against the intentional or unintentional advantage that the seller had acquired over the buyer overrode the policy to insure certainty in written agreements. The common law courts distinguished between two kinds of fraud—fraud in the execution and fraud in the inducement.[32]

Fraud in the execution arose where the party was justifiably unaware of what he had signed—for example, the situation where a blind person is told to sign a receipt. It later turns out that the paper is a sales agreement. The common law courts would not enforce this sales agreement because it had been procured by fraud. The blind man did not intend to sign a sales agreement, and thus a basic requirement was not met. The signing had come about because of the fraud practiced on the blind man.

Fraud in the execution was also available where an illiterate person signed a contract that he could not understand and therefore he could easily be misled. This defense was not extended to people who were not completely blind or completely illiterate. The usual theory was that people capable of reading ought to read what they are signing; and if they did not, they cannot argue that they were misled in the same fashion as a blind or illiterate person might have been. Justice Taft of the Ohio Supreme Court put it this way:

> A person of ordinary mind cannot say that he was misled into signing a paper which was different from what he intended to sign when he could have known the truth by merely looking when he signed. If this were permitted, contracts would not be worth the paper on which they are written. If a person can read and is not prevented from reading what he signs, he alone is responsible for his omission to read what he signs.[33] (Citation omitted.)

---

[31] Id. § 2-209(2) and Comment 3.

[32] See generally Annot., 56 A.L.R. 13 (1928).

[33] Dice v. Akron, C. & Y. R.R., 155 Ohio St. 185, 191, 98 N.E.2d 301, 304 (1951), rev'd on other grounds, 342 U.S. 359 (1952).

Hence, fraud in the execution was a way of getting around the parol evidence rule if the rather strict requirements could be shown. If this kind of fraud was shown, a court would declare the contract void.

Common law courts recognize a second kind of fraud—fraud in the inducement. Fraud in the inducement arose when a buyer knew or could easily find out that he was signing a sales agreement. Nonetheless, he signed the contract without ordinary investigation because of a false representation from the seller about the subject matter or content of the contract. If the buyer could establish this misrepresentation, his contract, though not void as was true in the fraud in the execution situation, was voidable and could be rescinded at the buyer's option. The parol evidence rule did not bar evidence of this kind of fraud.

An interesting example of rescission for fraud is a District of Columbia case, *Saylor v. Handley Motor Co.*[34] The buyer told an automobile dealer that he could only afford to pay eighty dollars per month for the purchase of his car. The seller assured him that the car he selected could be purchased for that sum. The buyer then signed a purchase agreement in which the monthly payments were left blank. Subsequently, the seller filled in these blank spaces, not for the agreed eighty dollars per month, but for the sum of eighty-eight dollars per month. The court held that this amounted to fraud on the buyer and permitted him to rescind the sales contract. The court pointed out in dictum that the rule was equally applicable to a sales agreement which was completed when the buyer signed it, but which contained terms that were contrary to the prior understanding of the parties. The court cited with approval the following language:

> The rule is that where one party to an oral agreement entrusts the other with the obligation of reducing it to writing, he has a right to rely upon the representation that it will be drawn accurately and in accordance with the oral understanding between them. The presentation of the paper for signature is in itself a representation that the terms of such oral agreement *have been or will be embodied in the writing.*[35] (Emphasis added.)

The court stated that fraud can occur even though the party is negligent in not reading the agreement before signing it where there is a false representation by the seller as to what is contained in the writing. Thus, under common law rules, oral warranties, which

---

[34] 169 A.2d 683 (D.C. Mun. Ct. App. 1961).
[35] *Id.* at 685.

were made by the seller and understood to be embodied in the written contract by the buyer, could provide a basis to rescind the agreement if they were not in fact so incorporated. However, the common law rule did not permit every written agreement to be ignored where there were prior oral agreements to the contrary. The whole purpose of the parol evidence rule was to prevent that from happening. To avoid the parol evidence rule, one had to show that he was induced to sign this writing because of the seller's false representation that something was contained in the agreement which actually was not there. The burden of proving the fraud is often a heavy one, requiring clear and convincing evidence. Moreover, the fact that the seller has a writing containing the buyer's signature is evidence suggesting that no fraud has been practiced.

Under the Code these common law distinctions and remedies remain. The actual words of the Code state that the parol evidence rules applies only to writings which are "intended by the parties as a final expression of their agreement. . . ."[36] If one party has been misled as to what the writing contains, it would seem the writing was not intended *by him* as any expression of his agreement, final or otherwise. Furthermore, the principles of "fraud, misrepresentation, duress, coercion, mistake, . . . or other validating or invalidating cause," found in section 1-103, supplement the sales provisions of the Code unless specifically displaced by it. The Code recognizes that fraud is available as a defense to a sales contract.[37] In fact, where fraud has been practiced in a sales situation, the buyer may exercise his common law right to rescind the contract.[38] In addition, section 2-721 also declares that all of the traditional remedies for damages provided by the Code are available to the buyer as well. Thus, a choice of remedies is provided to escape an agreement tainted by fraud.[39]

### III. UNCONSCIONABILITY AND GOOD FAITH

The Code permits a court to refuse to enforce a contract, or any part of it, which is unconscionable.[40] It is profitable to consider the prohibition on unconscionable agreements together with the duty to bargain in good faith imposed by the Code on all persons who enter

---

[36] U.C.C. § 2-202.
[37] *Id.* § 2-721.
[38] *Id.*
[39] *See* Associated Hardware Supply Co. v. Big Wheel Distrib. Co., 355 F.2d 114 (3d Cir. 1966).
[40] U.C.C. § 2-302(1).

into commercial transactions.[41] The Code establishes two tests for good faith. Nonmerchants must act honestly in a subjective sense.[42] However, section 2-103(1)(b) holds a merchant to a higher and more objective standard of good faith. A merchant has a duty to observe the reasonable commercial standards of fair dealing in his trade.[43] Fair dealing may be a higher standard of conduct than unconscionability. Certainly few trade associations would admit that their conception of fair dealing is measured only by standards of outright unconscionability. Most trades would probably assert that a great deal more is expected from their members in order to measure up to acceptable standards of fair dealing. Assuming a higher standard for the particular trade, when a merchant overreaches the standard of "fair dealing" in his trade, but has not reached the point of outright unconscionability, a buyer could argue that the transaction should be invalidated. However, no court has yet accepted the collective opinion of a trade as a basis for establishing the reasonable commercial standard of fair dealing to which an individual member of that trade should be held accountable.

## IV. LIMITATION OF REMEDY

Before the Code, a seller could try to avoid liability to a buyer by limiting the remedy available to the buyer in the original sales agreement.[44] The seller may concede that he has given an express warranty, or an implied warranty, or both of them. In fact, the seller may also admit that the warranties which were given have been breached. However, the seller then points to a clause in the sales agreement which states that the buyer's remedy for the breach of warranty is limited. For example, a liquidated damage clause in the sales agreement may limit recovery for a breach to a fixed sum of money insufficient to replace the buyer's actual losses. A sales agree-

---

41 *Id.* § 1-203.

42 *Id.* § 1-201(19) and Comment 19. This section defines good faith as honesty in fact. *See, e.g.*, Meadowbrook Nat'l Bank v. Markos, 3 U.C.C. RPTG. SERV. 854, 856 (N.Y. Sup. Ct. 1966).

43 U.C.C. § 2-103(1)(b).

44 *See, e.g.*, McDonald Credit Service, Inc. v. Church, 49 Wash. 2d 400, 301 P.2 1082 (1956); W. F. Dollen & Sons v. Carl R. Miller Tractor Co., 214 Iowa 774, 241 N.W. 307 (1932). *Cf.* SALES ACT § 71. *See generally* Fritz, *"Underliquidated" Damages as Limitation of Liability*, 33 TEXAS L. REV. 196, 196-98 (1954); Note, *Contractual Disclaimers of Warranty*, 23 MINN. L. REV. 784, 784-85 (1939) (containing a brief history of the use of disclaimers); Note, *Limitations On Freedom To Modify Contract Remedies*, 72 YALE L.J. 723, 724-26 (disclaimers), 746-55 (liquidated damages) (1963).

ment might provide that the seller shall not be liable at all for money damages, but provide for some kind of substitute remedy. For example, a substitute remedy might limit a buyer to a replacement of defective parts.

The Code's basic approach to contractual remedies is the authorize only fair and conscionable limitations of remedy. It contains a series of rules which declare certain specific kinds of limitations on remedies to be unfair and invalid.[45] Beyond these specific rules, the general doctrine of unconscionability may also invalidate grossly unfair remedy limitations.

One of these specific rules controls liquidated damage clauses.[46] Liquidated damage clauses can work two ways. First, the *buyer* may be required to pay a certain fixed sum of money if he does not perform the contract. The Code's approach to this problem is to codify the pre-Code law. When such a liquidated damage clause is unreasonably large compared to the actual damages suffered or anticipated the clause may be void as a penalty.[47] The second type of liquidated damage clause limits the seller's liability to less than he otherwise would have been responsible for under general rules of damages. For example, a seller who sells a washing machine to a buyer might provide that damages for breach of warranty shall not exceed five dollars even though the loss to a buyer is a great deal more than that. Since the limitation is entirely unreasonable in light of the anticipated or actual harm, the Code will invalidate this clause. If the liquidated damage clause is invalidated, the injured party may then proceed under normal Code rules for proving damages.

The Code has another section of specific rules dealing with substitute remedies.[48] One situation in which this section is useful is that where the sales agreement states that the buyer's only remedy for receiving defective goods is to have them replaced with satisfactory goods. The Code's first rule on this kind of clause is a technical one. If a particular substitute remedy is to be the exclusive remedy in lieu of the usual Code remedies, section 2-719 requires that the exclusive feature of the remedy be expressly stated in the sales agreement. If it is not expressly stated, the Code declares that the substitute remedy is only optional and in no way prevents an aggrieved party from pursuing all the other remedies normally given

---

45 U.C.C. §§ 2-718, 2-719.
46 *Id.* § 2-718.
47 *Id.* § 2-718(1) and Comment 1.
48 *Id.* § 2-719.

to him by the Code.[49] Even where the sales agreement does expressly state that the limited remedy is an exclusive one, such term may not be binding. If the essential purpose of the remedy should fail, the aggrieved party can ignore it and turn to his usual Code remedies instead.[50] For example, if a seller has sold a washing machine to a buyer and the sales agreement provides that the buyer's exclusive remedy shall be limited to a replacement of the defective parts, this limitation might appear to be a perfectly proper one. However, if the washing machine is poorly engineered and as a result every time it is used the motor burns out, this would seem to be a case where the exclusive or limited remedy has failed of its essential purpose, namely, the purpose of giving to the buyer a workable washing machine. Section 2-719 would then declare that this limitation on the remedy may be ignored and permit the buyer to turn to the other remedies normally provided for him under the Code, such as damages or revocation of acceptance.

Elements of fraud and misrepresentation may also remove the mandatory nature of an express limited remedy clause. In a recent California decision, the court dealt with seeds purchased by a tomato grower.[51] At the time of the sale, the seller knew that the tomato seeds were defective and would not produce high quality crops as warranted. His attempt to limit the remedy to return of purchase price was held to be a fraud on the buyer, which the buyer could ignore. The decision suggested that the limitation on the remedy might be ignored and the full damages recovered.[52] At least this would be so if the seller knew at the time of the sale that his goods were defective. According to the California court, if a seller knows when he sells his goods that they are defective, it is a fraud to limit the remedy. If this kind of rule is applicable in commercial situations, it seems that it ought to be equally applicable in consumer situations where a buyer is placed in an inequitable situation by limitations on remedies and the seller knew at the time of the sale that his goods would not work properly.

There is still another rule the Code imposes on an attempt to limit the remedies available for breach of warranty. The Code makes any attempt to limit damages for personal injury where consumer goods are involved prima facie unconscionable.[53] An examp'e of how

---

49 *Id.* § 2-719(1)(b).
50 *Id.* § 2-719(2).
51 Klein v. Asgrow Seed Co., 246 Cal. App. 2d 87, 54 Cal. Rptr. 609 (1966).
52 *Id.* at 98, 54 Cal. Rptr. at 617-19 (dictum).
53 U.C.C. § 2-719(3).

this might work would be where a housewife buys an iron and is severely burned because of a defect in the iron. The original sales agreement for the iron might have stated that no damages would be allowed by reasons of defects in the iron but instead limited the buyer's remedy to a refund of the purchase price, or to a replacement of the defective iron with a new one. However, because the iron is consumer goods and personal injuries are involved, the Code states that attempts by the seller to limit his buyer's remedy are prima facie unconscionable. Unless the seller can overcome this prima facie rule against him, the housewife may recover the full damages for her burns, regardless of the language of the sales agreement stating otherwise. This prima facie unconscionability rule where consumer goods are involved is of great interest to personal injury lawyers because automobiles are classified as consumer goods.

## V. EXCLUSION OF WARRANTIES

The seller may try to deny the existence of all warranties by a contract. If his goods are defective, the seller's limitation may be struck down if it comes within the spirit of the unconscionability doctrine which pervades all aspects of a sales transaction. It seems rather curious that Article 2 contains so many specific rules dealing with seller's attempts to *limit* the remedy for breach of warranty but provides only the general unconscionability doctrine to deal with a seller's attempt to completely exclude all warranties. Section 2-316 (1), however, prefers warranty-creating language over negating or limiting language when they cannot reasonably be construed as consistent.

## VI. EXCESSIVE PRICE

Another area in which unconscionability doctrine may prove helpful is where the price is excessive even though the goods are in no way defective. Several decisions strongly hint that excessive price alone may make a contract unconscionable. However, these decisions give little specific guidance to the problem of determining when, if ever, unconscionability can occur solely because the price is excessive.

The case most often discussed is *Williams v. Walker-Thomas Furniture Co.*[54] From 1957 to 1962 the appellants purchased a number of household items from the Walker-Thomas Furniture Company. At the time of each purchase the appellants signed a form contract which purported to lease the additional items to them for

---

[54] 350 F.2d 445 (D.C. Cir. 1965).

a monthly rental payment. The title to each item was to remain in the furniture company until all the monthly payments were made. This add-on provision had the effect of maintaining title in Walker-Thomas until all the outstanding lease payments were made on each purchase. Among the items was a stereo with a purchase price of 678 dollars, which was sold to appellants while they were receiving public assistance payments. Walker-Thomas knew appellants were receiving public assistance. On default by appellants Walker-Thomas sought to repossess the stereo, along with almost all of the other household furniture purchased by appellants during the 1957 to 1962 period.[55]

In his defense to repossession, the buyer argued "unconscionability." The trial court criticised the sharp practice and irresponsible business policy of selling high-priced stereo sets to welfare recipients, but felt compelled to hold for the seller on the grounds that the doctrine of unconscionability was not part of the common law.[56] The court of appeals reversed, holding that unconscionability was a defense available at common law. The court remanded the case, directing the trial court to determine whether unconscionability actually existed under the facts of this case.[57] The disposition on remand was apparently not reported.

The precedent that *Walker-Thomas* established was that an action based on a theory of unconscionability could be maintained without statute. Since the subsequent adoption of the Code in the District of Columbia there is little need for this authority. The case did not define the elements needed for a successful action based on unconscionability or what remedy would be available. The problem of fashioning a remedy may be a difficult one. Would this court permit the buyer to keep the stereo set without paying for it or give the buyer an absolute right to return the set and recover any payments? The implications of the decision on consumer sales raises serious policy questions. Did this court mean to suggest that sellers are supposed to police their poor-risk customers and determine what goods they may or may not buy? Did the court mean to imply that welfare recipients may not purchase stereo sets, or other luxury or semi-luxury items?[58] If so, would they be equally barred from buying

---

55 *Id.* at 445-447.

56 *Id.* at 448-449.

57 *Id.* at 450.

58 *Cf.* Leff, *Unconscionability and the Code—the Emperor's New Clothes*, 115 U. PA. L. REV. 485, 558 (1967) arguing that the low income consumer should be discouraged from purchasing luxury goods.

a small table radio, which, perhaps, is not a necessity of life but gives great pleasure to it? What does this kind of a decision do to the availability of credit to these buyers? If the implications of this decision are carried to their fullest, just what legitimate seller will deal with impoverished buyers, even at a fair price, where the possibility exists that if he does so, a court might second guess him on his decision to deal with this buyer? The *Walker-Thomas* case provides little insight into the specific characteristics of unconscionability and leaves many vague suggestions which, if carried to their ultimate, could prove disturbing. The dissenting opinion pointed out that this buyer apparently knew her obligations when she entered into the sale; and, that if overseeing of welfare clients' purchases is required, then it should come through a legislative program and not by judicial fiat.[59]

A more useful case is *American Home Improvement, Inc. v. MacIver*.[60] That case involved a sale of siding, fourteen windows and one door. The actual cost of installation was about 950 dollars; however, added to this cost was a sales commission of 800 dollars and carrying charges for a sixty-month period of another 800 dollars. The buyer signed a contract to pay about 2,500 dollars for only 950 dollars worth of goods. The New Hampshire court found this to be unconscionable and refused to enforce the contract.[61] The persuasive force of this case may suffer due to the rather unusual position of the parties at the time the action was brought. The buyer had cancelled the contract after the seller had completed a negligible amount of work. Accordingly, a complete cancellation of the contract could be ordered by a court without causing any undue hardship to the seller or any unjust enrichment to the buyer. A much more difficult situation arises when the goods have been delivered to the buyer and used by him. Since the *American Home Improvement* case did not deal with this kind of fact situation, it could easily be distinguished in the more typical situation where the contract has been executed. A further limitation on the applicability of *American Home Improvement* is that the contract at issue was in violation of the New Hampshire truth-in-lending statute.[62] Thus, a ground for decision independent of the unconscionability issue existed, and the court held

---

59 350 F.2d at 450 (dissenting opinion).
60 105 N.H. 435, 201 A.2d 886 (1964).
61 *Id.* at 438-39, 201 A.2d at 888-89.
62 *Id.* at 437-38, 201 A.2d at 887.

the contract unenforceable both because it violated the New Hampshire disclosure statute and because it was unconscionable.

The case which most strongly supports the proposition that excessive price alone may make a contract unconscionable in *Frostifresh Corp. v. Reynoso.*[63] The facts present the more typical situation where the contract has been executed by delivery and use of the goods. The sale involved a refrigerator-freezer with a cash price of 900 dollars and added carrying charges of 246 dollars, making the total purchase price 1,145 dollars. The seller admitted that the appliance had cost him 348 dollars. The buyer defaulted on his payments, but maintained possession of the appliance. The seller then sought damages for breach of contract. The trial court held that the transaction was unconscionable and limited the seller's recovery to his wholesale price, instead of the normal retail price.[64] The decision was reversed as to the remedy with the statement that

> while the evidence clearly warrants a finding that the contract was unconscionable (UCC § 2-302), we are of the opinion that plaintiff should recover its net cost for the refrigerator-freezer, plus a reasonable profit, in addition to trucking and services charges incurred and reasonable finance charges.[65]

The appellate court did not specify its reasons for holding that the facts presented a clear case of unconscionability. The evidence showed, in addition to the excessive price, that the buyers were Spanish-speaking persons who could not understand English.[66] As such, they had no way of reading or understanding the sales contract which was written in English, and the seller made an effort to avoid translating or explaining the document to them.

Another case which purports to hold a contract unenforceable because the purchase price was excessive is *In re State of New York ex rel Lefkowitz v. ITM, Inc.*[67] ITM Inc. had devised an elaborate sales routine which involved alleged misrepresentations and fraudulent sales practices. The "buyers" were induced to sign the retail installment payment contracts by a plan through which the purchaser was to be paid for referring prospective customers to ITM. The trial court held that the contracts were unconscionable and therefore

---

63 52 Misc. 2d 26, 274 N.Y.S.2d 757 (Dist. Ct. 1966), *rev'd as to remedy* 54 Misc. 2d 119, 281 N.Y.S.2d 964 (App. Div. 1967).

64 *Id.* at 28, 274 N.Y.S.2d at 760.

65 54 Misc. 2d 119, 120, 281 N.Y.S.2d 964, 965 (App. Div. 1967).

66 52 Misc. 2d 26, 27, 274 N.Y.S.2d 757, 758 (Dist. Ct. 1966).

67 52 Misc. 2d 39, 275 N.Y.S.2d 303 (Sup. Ct. Trial Term 1966).

unenforceable. However, the court also found that ITM, Inc. was guilty of fraudulent practices, that the scheme was an illegal lottery, and that the contracts were unenforceable because ITM, Inc. was an unlicensed foreign corporation.[68] *ITM* is another example of a court using unconscionability language in conjunction with other elements of unfairness, or alternative grounds of decision. The court held that even if the prices were not unconscionable *per se,* they were excessive in the context of the case.[69]

From these cases dealing with the unconscionability doctrine as applied to excessive price, it seems fairly clear that excessive price coupled with other factors, such as a purely executory contract or a foreign-speaking purchaser who did not understand the contract, has served as a basis for finding unconscionability. Whether excessive price alone is enough has not yet been established. Of course, minor discrepancies between actual price and true value will probably never be enough to bring about a finding of unconscionability. More likely, something approaching a "shocking" discrepancy will be required. German law uses a price-value differential of one-half as a measure of unconscionability[70] and most American cases seem to require at least that much of a disparity.[71]

At present price-value disparity alone is probably not enough to establish unconscionability of a sales contract. The Uniform Consumer Credit Code suggests the court should consider the circumstances giving rise to the price-value disparity.[72] While this Code has not yet been promulgated by the National Conference of Commissioners on Uniform State Laws, and probably will not be for the next year or so,* it may provide some insight as to where future legislation on this problem may be headed. Briefly, where excessive price is involved, the test for unconscionability adopted by the Uniform Consumer Credit Code looks for a "gross disparity" between the price paid and the price readily obtainable by buyers of similar credit in a credit transaction in the same area. In other words, the Uniform Consumer Credit Code does not look at the price-value disparity alone; it also looks at the buyer involved.[73] Apparently, it

---

[68] *Id.* at 62, 275 N.Y.S.2d at 329-30.

[69] *Id.* at 53, 275 N.Y.S.2d at 321.

[70] 78 HARV. L. REV. 895, 898 (1965).

[71] *See* Skilton and Helstad, *Protection of the Installment Buyer of Goods under the Uniform Commercial Code,* 65 MICH. L. REV. 1465, 1475 (1967).

[72] UNIFORM CONSUMER CREDIT CODE § 6.111 (Tent. Draft No. 6, 1967).

[73] *Id.* § 6.111(3)(c).

\* Prof. Shanker's remarks were made in 1967. The U3C was recently promulgated. —ED.

would recognize that the credit worthiness of some buyers is so
much less than the credit worthiness of other buyers that higher
prices can lawfully be charged to take care of the seller's higher
risk. It is only when the higher price presents gross disparity from
what a particular buyer could normally have obtained elsewhere
that unconscionability might result.

The test found in the Uniform Consumer Credit Code is similar
to that used recently by a Pennsylvania federal district court in *In re
Elkins-Dell.*[74] Unconscionability, Judge Lord pointed out in his
opinion, is not proven merely by a showing that the terms are oner-
ous, oppressive, or one-sided. Instead, it must be shown that the terms
bear no reasonable relationship to the business risks involved in the
transaction. Judge Lord implied the ability of the debtor to obtain
more favorable credit terms elsewhere was relevant to the issue of
unconscionability.[75]

The *Elkins-Dell* case arose from an involuntary bankruptcy proceeding. Prior to the initiation of the bankruptcy proceedings Fidel-
ity American Financial Corporation executed a loan to Elkins-Dell
taking an assignment of accounts receivable. When the question of
enforceability was presented to the court, twenty-four thousand
dollars in accounts receivable would have been included in the
bankrupt's estate if the contract were held to be unconscionable.
The referee so found, but the district court remanded the case for
further findings of fact.[76]

> The ultimate question for the referee will be whether these con-
> tracts were, in the light of all the circumstances, reasonable com-
> mercial devices. Among the issues which may be explored . . .
> are the financial positions of the bankrupts at the time the
> agreements were entered into; the extent to which agreements
> of this kind are customary among lenders like Fidelity; the
> extent to which Fidelity's contracts vary with and reflect antici-
> pated risks; the availability of other credit to the bankrupts, both
> at the time and after they entered into these agreements; the
> extent to which the various provisions were enforced by Fidelity
> or influenced the bankrupt's business conduct, particularly their
> ability to secure other funds; whether the terms of these con-
> tracts facilitated commerce by making funds available where
> they otherwise would not be or impeded commerce by preclud-
> ing access to other sources of funds. . . .[77]

---

74 *In re* Matter of Elkins-Dell Mfg. Co., 253 F. Supp. 864 (E.D. Pa. 1966).
75 *Id.*
76 *Id.* at 875.
77 *Id.* at 874.

The court also held that the referee should consider the impact of his decision or future financing in similar situations.[78]

*Elkins-Dell* gives approval to the notion that unconscionability where price and credit are involved cannot be based on price alone but must also take into consideration the capacity of a particular buyer to get better credit elsewhere. This may be a severe limitation on the usefulness of the unconscionability doctrine to those persons who are so impoverished that they often suffer the most unfair contracts, because many of these buyers could not have gotten credit elsewhere, or at least not on any better terms.

### SUMMARY

In this article the authors have tried to explore consumer protection devices found in the U.C.C. and the special problems they create. Although many of the consumer remedies discussed have not yet been clearly defined, or in some cases even recognized, by the courts, they are available to the lawyer who may represent the consumer. The discussion does not purport to be complete, but an outline of the path in which the law may develop toward greater protection of the consumer. The large number of recent cases in the area indicates that the development of the law, within the general framework created by the U.C.C., has just begun.

---

[78] *Id.* at 875.

# INCREASING LOW-INCOME CONSUMER BUYING AND BORROWING POWER BY COOPERATIVE ACTION†

MERLIN G. MILLER*

Cooperative action, in the broadest sense of the term, is an ingredient in most, if not all, community action. A Community Chest campaign, for example, involves the voluntary participation and organized activity of a large number of workers, and the participation of a still larger number of contributors. This is a very important kind of cooperation, recognized and approved by sociologists and ordinary citizens alike.

The cooperative activity by which low-income consumers can raise their purchasing power and their borrowing power is of a different order. In the first place, theirs is a business enterprise, not a philanthrophic activity. Although it has important sociological overtones, it is primarily an economic activity. In the second place, the individuals participating all expect to be beneficiaries of the activity in which they participate. They look upon themselves, or should look upon themselves as receivers as well as givers, recipients in proportion to their own contribution and participation. The essence of this participation is mutual self-help.

This paper is, therefore, concerned with cooperation in this narrow sense. In a still narrower sense it is concerned with those types of cooperative enterprise most useful to the poor consumer. These cooperatives of, by and for the poor, are here analyzed for the lawyer who is only casually informed on the subject of cooperatives. The author is not himself a lawyer but is a long-time cooperative organizer and educator. Let us begin, then, to determine exactly what is meant by the term " a cooperative."

## I. WHAT IS A COOPERATIVE?

There are many superficial answers. To a New Yorker a cooperative is a high-rise apartment building owned by the tenants. To

---

† This article is an expansion of an address given by Mr. Miller at a seminar on law and poverty in Columbus, Ohio in 1967, first published in OHIO ST. LEGAL SERVICES ASS'N, THE COURSE ON LAW AND POVERTY: THE CONSUMER (1967). [used by permission. ED.]

* Consultant in cooperative education and economic development, Economic Opportunity Dept., Cooperative League of the U.S.A.; formerly coordinator of field training, Board of Cooperative Training, Inc. and Cooperative Training Center, University of Wisconsin (1962-65).

a grain farmer from Kansas a cooperative is a tall grain elevator with the word CO-OP in bold letters across the top. Neither is entirely incorrect. "Cooperative" is used commonly—and loosely—to describe a business enterprise operated on a cooperative basis. Still more loosely it is used to describe the business buildings and facilities of such an enterprise. But in its essence, a cooperative is a group of people who have joined together to carry on a business enterprise for the benefit of all of them. The cooperative enterprise is one which provides services which the cooperators cannot individually provide for themselves as well as they can by acting together.

There are three ways of defining "cooperative": first, the basic, sociological definition which refers to the group jointly operating a business enterprise; second, the economic—and legal—definition which is concerned with the enterprise itself as a legal entity; and third, the looser figure of speech applied, by metonymy, to the buildings and other physical facilities associated with the business enterprise. It is the second type of definition which we need here: Let us say a cooperative is a self-help, user-owned, group business enterprise. Every word of this functional definition is important: *self-help, user-owned, group business enterprise.*

## II. THE INFINITE VARIETY OF COOPERATIVES

Almost any kind of business enterprise can be organized on a cooperative basis. A variety of cooperatives have been organized recently in the South, as an aftermath of the civil rights movement there. These include sewing cooperatives, a small garment factory, a bakery, a woodworking plant and a sweet potato marketing cooperative. In the ghettos of northern cities there are buying clubs, a dress shop, day care centers, credit unions, a super-market and even a discotheque. All are owned by the poor and operated on a cooperative basis for the benefit of the poor.

Around the world the variety of cooperatives is almost limitless. There are cooperatives of shoemakers in Mexico and Honduras. There are cooperatives of the blind and the handicapped which produce handicrafts and electronic components in Poland. There is a cooperative in Burma which captures and tames wild elephants. There are fishermen's cooperatives on every ocean and sea of the world. The infinite variety of economic activity which can be undertaken by people who want to help themselves is a challenge to their legal advisers to use imagination and to discover new subjects for cooperation.

### III. The Difficulties of Organizing Cooperatives Among the Poor

When considering the bewildering variety of possible cooperative enterprises, it is wise to go back to the definition of a cooperative: a business enterprise organized by a group of people on a self-help and user-owned basis. Look at each separate part of that definition and it becomes clear that those who organize cooperatives among the poor face difficulties that most businesses never face.

The first element of a cooperative is *self-help*. There is some truth in the oft-repeated generalizations that the poor are poor because by and large they are uneducated, even illiterate, apathetic or unambitious. In some quarters there is also an element of fear—fear of the loss of a job or of being evicted from a home. And finally there is a long dependence upon various forms of welfare and relief. No one of these handicaps applies to all of the poor; and there are some who have none of these handicaps. However, it is generally true that cooperative self-help presents difficult organizational problems among the poor. That means there has to be a well planned program, involving gradually increasing information, education—in the action sense of that word—and self-reliance before any group can successfully organize on a self-help basis. They are the people least capable of effective self-help. Yet a cooperative is essentially a group whose members pull themselves up by their own bootstraps. If the enterprise is run by somebody else for the poor it may be welfare or charity, but certainly it is not a cooperative.

The second element of a cooperative is *user-ownership*—the people that use the business own it. By definition the poor lack capital. Nevertheless user-ownership is impossible without the investment by the prospective members of some risk capital. The prospective cooperator must understand the necessity for the risk. No lawyer or other counselor should permit anyone he advises to join a cooperative under the assumption he will receive something for nothing. He will first give his patronage, and pay for the food, appliances, medical services or whatever he acquires through the cooperative. He also must make an investment—a capital investment. The poor today must do the same thing the poor have always done when organizing cooperatives: they must put in a little money of their own. They must leave money in the business if it is to be a successful cooperative. This is true even though outside agencies may initially provide much more capital than the cooperators themselves do. The prospective cooperator must accept the risk of "going into business" if he is going to be a true cooperator. Investment and patronage are the two assets that a cooperative must have to succeed.

The other side of the coin must also be recognized. Many kinds of cooperatives of the poor will need, in addition to the members' pennies or dollars, large amounts of capital investment from outside sources if they are to get off the ground at all.

Third, a cooperative is a *group enterprise*. Confidence and mutual trust are the foundations of ordinary business transactions in our society. If a businessman could not trust another's word, check, telephone order or price quotation, our vaunted corporate business structure and our affluent society would be quite different. Confidence and mutual trust are even more significant in the democratic corporate structure of the cooperative. This is especially true among the poor, who have so little to lose, and to whom that little means so much.

The poor weavers of Rochdale, the originators of the worldwide cooperative movement, saved their money, some of them only a penny a week, for a full year. They entrusted those meager savings to one person, their treasurer, a year before they could go into business and expend their savings for their first small stock of goods. The Raifeissen Credit Societies started among poor farmers of Germany about the same time; they were organized on the basis of unlimited liability. They saved their money in a society which could loan the money to any member who needed it. If he did not pay back the loan, all the members of the society were liable. Such is the foundation of trust upon which cooperatives started in a day when no government aid was available. The poor in our cities have been conditioned to be wary and suspicious. They distrust the stranger and the outsider who has a place of business in their immediate vicinity. These suspicions can only be overcome by dynamic and trustworthy leadership, patient and continuous education, and small steps, one at a time, in cooperative action.

There is a fourth factor in the definition of a cooperative organized among the poor under the provisions of the Economic Opportunity Act. It is not only a self-help, user-owned, group business enterprise. It is an *aided* cooperative. Many kinds of assistance are available under the Economic Opportunity Act. Grants may be obtained for developing an organizational base for cooperative programs and for the conduct and administration of these programs in their initial stages. There can be payment for advice and assistance of specialists, technicians and consultants and grants for training personnel needed in cooperative programs. There can be loans to cooperatives for furnishing essential services. This last is particularly true in the rural areas through the Farmers Home Administration.[1]

The terms *aided* and *self-help* seem to be contradictory. They are not; they do go together. We all know that there is no such thing as a truly self-made man. We all get assistance in development of our own characters, business enterprises, careers and professional skills. So do cooperatives, even the most prosperous middle class cooperatives. The Hyde Park Cooperative Society in Chicago began as a little buying club which met and did business in one room of a private home. It now does six million dollars business annually and is the largest food store in Chicago. Individuals gave time without pay to carry on this business in the Depression years. In the initial stages of most of the now prosperous farmers' cooperatives in the Middle West there were persons and organizations contributing time and energy without pay. Today, it is even more true that most cooperatives among the poor must begin with aided self-help. It is difficult to obtain aid at all. To do so at the correct time and maintain business progress requires skill and diplomacy. There is another pitfall: the assistance must not be too great. It must not be so much as to kill the cooperators' sense of self-achievement.

## IV. The Legal Structure of Cooperatives

It is possible for a small cooperative to operate for a time without being incorporated. But it is desirable for a newly formed group to have a lawyer advise that this involves certain hazards. As long as a buying club is unincorporated, every person placing an order to be delivered at a later date is gambling when he prepays that order. If the treasurer absconds before the next meeting there is not much recourse. Remaining unincorporated has the advantage of impressing upon all the members that they are dependent on each other, not upon Uncle Sam nor their lawyer. They must make it on their own and they must trust each other. The establishment of mutual trust in a cooperate group may mean the difference between the members of that group staying in th disadvantaged class and being on the road upward.

Generally, it is not necessary to incorporate a cooperative when the business is a simple one, perhaps just one service provided to a few members. As the business becomes more complex and serves

---

1 These and other aids available are described in Cooperative League of the USA and Office of Economic Opportunity, Moving Ahead With Cooperatives (1967).

more members, the cooperative must either be incorporated or abandoned. Otherwise the operation is likely to become unwieldy, its structure disintegrate, and its rules be amended out of existence. The more rigid structure required by law is conducive to stability and good management as well as a valuable limitation on personal liability.

When the day to incorporate arrives, it is important to know the essential differences between a cooperative and an ordinary business corporation. There are four distinctive features which every member of a cooperative should understand.

First, the cooperative is *organized under non-profit laws.* The laws require that the application for a charter specifically state that the cooperative is organized "not for profit."[2]

The second feature is the implementation in a business enterprise of the "not-for-profit" restriction: the dividend, if any, paid on the members' shares of stock must be *strictly limited.*[3] In practice this means the return on investment in a cooperative is limited to an amount equivalent to a modest rate of interest. If a cooperative is successful it does "make money." In the bookkeeping sense it has "profit." But there is a sharp distinction between the accounting profit and the concept used in denominating a corporation "non-profit." As used in defining both eleemosynary corporations and cooperatives, that term means neither the organizers of, the officers in, the contributors to nor the members of the organization shall share in any monies received from its philanthropic or business operations. The "non-profit" definition as applied to a cooperative requires that the money made on transactions shall not be distributed to the members as investors at a rate that is any higher than they could have gotten as interest if they have made a loan to the cooperative. The statutory language may vary from jurisdiction to jurisdiction, but the principle is universal, and it is exceedingly important.[4]

The limitation on distribution as dividends of earnings or savings makes it possible for the cooperative earnings or savings to be returned to the members as *users* in proportion to their use of the business. This return to users is the third and most distinctive feature of the cooperative: the *patronage refund* principle. This principle does not require that the members take their earnings out of the business. If they desire to devote their savings to social or community

---

2 *E.g.*, D.C. CODE ANN. § 29-801(1) (1967).

8 *Id.* § 29-822.

4 *Id.* § 29-831(2).

uses such as a playground, they are perfectly free to do so under most cooperative laws.[5] But if they do vote to "take their earnings out" they must be distributed in proportion to volume of business done with the cooperative.[6]

The fourth distinctive feature is the principle of *democratic control*. This requirement, often stated as "one member, one vote," is in all consumer cooperative laws.[7] It is the direct antithesis of the ordinary or profit corporate practice which gives each stockholder as many votes as he has shares. In cooperatives, it is men not money that control.

There are, of course, many other requirements for incorporation under the cooperative laws. Some states have no laws for consumer cooperatives at all. Ohio has a detailed "Cooperative Marketing Act" for farmers' cooperatives[8] but only one section on consumers' cooperatives.[9] It is advisable that cooperatives for low-income persons be incorporated in the District of Columbia.[10]

## V. INCREASING LOW-INCOME CONSUMER BUYING POWER: CONSUMER COOPERATIVES AND OTHER COOPERATIVE SERVICES

The term "consumer cooperative" tends to restrict our imagination. We think in terms of the food store, the supermarket. Food, to be sure, is the greatest necessity. It is well-documented that the poor pay more for food, and get poorer quality than do average middle-class Americans.[11] To meet this need by organizing a consumer cooperative food store as a first venture is a herculean, almost an impossible task. A successful supermarket requires hundreds of thousands of dollars of capital—an immense amount for the very poor. The cooperative supermarket must be in a position to compete with the most efficient of the chain stores with their multi-million dollar

---

5 *E.g., id.* §§ 29-822, 29-831(3).

6 *Id.* § 29-831(4). Provision is also often made for distribution of stock dividends in order to retain capital for expansion.

7 *E.g., id.* § 29-813. This section also provides that "No voting agreement or other device to evade the . . . rule shall be enforceable at law or in equity."

8 OHIO REV. CODE ANN., §§ 1729.01-.27 (Page 1953).

9 OHIO REV. CODE ANN., § 1729.28 (Page 1953).

10 D.C. CODE ANN. §§ 29-801—29-847 (1967). These sections are known as the District of Columbia Cooperative Association Act. In addition to the advantages mentioned above, the Act makes certain essentials to successful cooperation mandatory. Allocation for educational purposes and for a reserve fund are examples. Bonding is also required. Distribution of returns on capital are limited to fifty percent of paid up capital. In addition, directors must be members of the cooperative.

11 D. CAPLOVITZ, THE POOR PAY MORE (1963).

resources. Where people of very moderate means have organized successful cooperative food stores, one or more of the following factors has usually existed: operation in connection with a large cooperative housing project; organization as a branch or affiliate of an already going and sound middle-class cooperative; the infusion of considerable sums of capital from outside sources; or the technical help and guidance of the staff of one of the regional consumer cooperative wholesale federations.[12]

The cooperative food store is not the only type of cooperative that the poor can use to expand their buying power. The simplest approach to the problem of high food costs is the cooperative buying club. The small group who organize a buying club meet regularly to pool their orders which are purchased at wholesale. The buying club is strictly a self-help type of cooperative depending on the voluntary service of the members of the group. As a preliminary step to more extensive business development it is an excellent educational tool. "Save as you learn about business" might well be the motto.[13]

The cooperative foodstore can sometimes be organized most successfully in isolated communities. The CAG (Community Action Group) store in Gilbert Creek, West Virginia, is an example. Stimulated by the director of the local Economic Opportunity organization, retired mine workers, old age pensioners, welfare recipients and other low-income people of this remote community organized their own store at $10.00 a share. They have brought down prices, and built up their own hope and courage. Now they are talking of other cooperative action, possibly a credit union.[14]

This is typical of cooperative development. Where one venture succeeds, other cooperative services are apt to follow. There are many needs besides food that can be satisfied cooperatively. These cooperative services may be organized quite independently of a cooperative foodstore or buying club, or they may grow out of such cooperatives. Cooperative services which are springing up among low-income people include such diverse enterprises as an eye-care center, a discotheque organized and operated by the youth it serves, a day care center operated by mothers who are thereby enabled to

---

12 Information about such federations may be found in MOVING AHEAD WITH COOPERATIVES, *supra* note 1.

13 *See* THE COOPERATIVE LEAGUE, MOVING AHEAD WITH GROUP ACTION (1967).

14 CUNA International, "The Poor Don't Have to Pay More," *Everybody's Money*, Spring, 1967.

get remunerative jobs, and a discount drug buying service that cuts sharply the cost of medicines.

There are other services which can be provided at a savings. Insurance is one of these—where saving comes largely through group premiums. Burial service is another important service which can be obtained cooperatively. Admittedly it is difficult to get the extremely poor who are thinking about tomorrow's meals and paying for a television set or a washing machine to think ahead to that inevitable day when they or their families will be faced with the heavy expense of a funeral service. Successful cooperative action of the poor in the areas of insurance and burial services requires working closely with insurance companies and burial societies which are participating in the anti-poverty program.

Many of these valuable services to the poor can be combined through a business counseling service. Where low-income people undertake this service for themselves they are more free to bargain than are government or welfare agencies supported by public funds. Such a cooperatively owned and operated counseling service can save its members significant sums on their major purchases, showing them how they can buy certain appliances, for example, at much reduced prices from recommended businesses. This leads naturally to a sort of "bargaining association" and agreements with reputable businesses that are quite willing to deal with the poor if the transactions are cash, avoiding costly credit and the collection problems. A multi-service business advisory center which is organized cooperatively becomes, in effect, a discount house for the poor. They are the people who need such service most and now have least access to it.[15]

## VI. Increasing Consumer Borrowing Power: Credit Unions

Many of the kinds of purchases covered by the consumer and service cooperatives listed above are the kinds of purchases that, in our affluent society, are made most often on credit. Television sets, radios, washers, not to mention automobiles, are commonly purchased by middle-class people on credit. The poor, too, make such purchases on credit. This credit is often at outrageous rates, the purchases far beyond the buyer's means of repayment and the rate of defaults and repossessions very high. It is a sad commentary on our society that those who need credit the least are the ones to

---

15 For a thorough description of such special service cooperatives see H. SHADEN, JR., A MODEL CONSUMER ACTION PROGRAM FOR LOW INCOME NEIGHBORHOODS.

whom it is most freely available and on the most favorable terms. The converse is equally true, to the point that the credit system which is the very basis of our economy works in conformity with the ancient Christian observation "to him that hath shall be given and from him that hath not shall be taken away even what he seemeth to have."

To this problem of credit for the poor, the answer is *not* extension of credit by the various consumer cooperative enterprises. That runs so counter to the experience of consumer cooperatives that many consumer cooperators have regarded cash trading as an unalterable rule of true cooperation. The cooperative answer is the cooperative savings and loan association, an enterprise in which the owners are the depositors, and only they can borrow. In the United States these societies are known as credit unions, and they operate under very strict state or federal laws.[16] Many cooperators agree the credit union is the most fundamental of all cooperative organizations, the one that provides the most essential services to its members: encouraging thrift and savings, providing credit when needed, and developing financial independence and human dignity. It should not, however, be joined with another cooperative enterprise prior to the maturity of either.

Structurally the credit union is a financial institution which differs from a cooperative commercial or service enterprise in several ways. One of the most important of these differences is the necessity to organize it among a group of people with an existing common bond. The "field of membership," to use the common credit union terminology, may be employment in the same industry or institution, such as a steel mill, the post office or a school system. The common bond may also be membership in the same church, fraternal order, labor union, or cooperative; or residence in a small, well-defined rural community or town. The basic idea is that this financial institution, this "little people's bank" (it really isn't a bank) will be owned and controlled by those who know and trust each other. This is the basic safeguard for their tiny but highly important individual savings. It is also the basis upon which the credit union loans these savings prudently and at the same time generously for the urgent needs of its members.

The second difference between the credit union and the cooperative that deals in goods and services is in the "commodity"

---

16 12 U.S.C. §§ 1751 *et seq.* (1964); *e.g.*, D.C. CODE ANN. § 26-519 *et seq.* (1967), OHIO REV. CODE ANN. §§ 1733.01-.99 (Page Supp. 1967).

the credit union has to sell, which is "money." For this service the credit union, by law, can charge only a limited interest rate.[17] In passing it should be noted that the credit unions have a half-century record of doing what the new "truth in lending" laws require: making a complete disclosure in advance of the full costs of credit and the true annual interest rate. In the credit union the profit is returned pro-rata to members, for the most part not in proportion to their use of the business as borrowers, but in proportion to their investment in shares.[18] The primary "saving" to the member as borrower is the lower interest rate. The long range purpose of the credit union is to encourage thrift even though its immediate service is to provide loans at reasonable rates.

It is true that as a credit union and its members[19] prosper it may accumulate more money than its borrowing members need to borrow. It then becomes a part of mainstream America, where continued prosperity seems to depend on expanding credit. Such a credit union may reduce its interest rate to get all its members' money to "work", that is, on loan to borrowing members.

Although the long-range purpose of the credit union may be to encourage thrift and the practice of saving, most people join credit unions initially in order to borrow. This is especially true of credit unions of low-income persons. Indeed, many credit union leaders have felt that the accumulation of savings is so slow a process that the low-income credit union never could make enough significant loans to attract and hold members.

The first successes by American credit union organizers at work among the poor, significantly enough, began among the very poor in underdeveloped countries overseas. Experiences in Jamaica, Trinidad, the Fiji Islands, and a score of other countries taught some American credit union leaders that "where only pennies can be saved, only dollars will be borrowed." When the same low-key, long-term educational efforts were tried in the United States some remarkable successes were achieved. The story of the Guadelupe Organization Credit Union illustrates several aspects of the unique character of credit unions among low-income people.[19] It was organized among the residents of a community that had already dem-

---

17 *E.g.*, 12 U.S.C. § 1757(5) (1964); OHIO REV. CODE ANN. § 1733.08 (Page Supp. 1967).

18 Some credit unions give recognition to the patronage refund principle by annually refunding a portion of the interest paid by member-borrowers during the year.

19 CUNA International, "The Impact of Self-Help," *Credit Union Magazine*, May, 1966, pp. 8-13.

onstrated the power of people organized and working together. Through their Guadelupe Organization they had already secured health services, street lights, police protection and many other services. They were closely associated with the state Credit Union League. Their credit union is located in the community service building where many related services are available. Most important, it was organized and is staffed by trusted local leaders.

A recent development in the war on poverty is the attempt to find ways to provide additional capital to loan to the members of a new credit union among the poor which has very little money of its own to loan. In Milwaukee, where Wisconsin law allows a broad interpretation of the "bond of membership,"[20] the Wisconsin State Central Credit Union has opened a branch for low-income members in a predominantly Spanish community. In Michigan, where the state law allows one credit union to join and become a member of another credit union,[21] a number of strong credit unions have "joined" three new credit unions in low-income housing projects. Each of the strong credit unions has made an initial capital "deposit" of a thousand dollars, thus enabling the new credit union to start with about 10,000 dollars available for loans. These experiments in providing initial capital for new credit unions of low-income members may provide a pattern for wise borrowing, habits of saving and eventually financial independence for even the poor. To determine what is possible in a given state, one should consult the state credit union league, or the national association known as CUNA International.[22]

## VII. IMPROVED HOUSING BY COOPERATIVE ACTION

Housing is not usually placed in the same category as food, household supplies and credit as a consumer need which the poor can meet by cooperative action. Food and credit are daily or short-term needs; housing is long-term. Buying a home involves the largest purchase, and the biggest debt most families ever undertake. Moreover, housing is generally recognized as one of the three basic problems of the ghettos, the other two being limited education and under-employment.

There are cooperative means of meeting the problems of hous-

---

20 WIS. STAT. ANN. § 186.09 (Supp. 1968).

21 MICH. COMP. LAWS § 490.4(d) (1967).

22 CUNA International, P.O. Box 431, Madison, Wisconsin 53701 (formerly Credit Union National Association). It serves credit unions in the United States and Canada and in a score of other countries around the globe.

ing. A portion of urban society has found very great savings in cooperative apartment construction and ownership. The movement began in America when Abraham Kazan developed the first cooperative apartment project for members of the International Ladies Garment Workers Union, and other laborers as well. From that beginning has grown a whole galaxy of cooperatively-owned highrise apartments in New York City, each apartment complex owned and operated by its tenants and each affiliated with the parent promotional and service organization, the United Housing Foundation.[23] These cooperative apartments have been financed through small down payments by the prospective tenant-owners and substantial mortgage investment by sponsoring unions, banks and insurance companies.

Cooperative ownership and finance has reduced the cost of construction, management services, maintenance and monthly carrying charges to approximately eighty percent of the amounts paid as rental in similar privately owned apartments. In addition, these cooperatively owned communities have provided the climate for the development of cooperative supermarkets, drug stores, day care centers and insurance service.

Section 213 of the National Housing Act[24] is the federal Magna Charta of cooperative housing. Under this legislation, the Federal Housing Administration has written 1.6 billion dollars of mortgage insurance, with less loss than on any other type of multi-family housing. Most of the projects insured have been urban or suburban cooperative apartments for middle-income residents.

These "213 cooperatives" have been aided by a strong promotional and service organization, the Foundation for Cooperative Housing, and its operating subsidiary, the FCH Company.[25] The latter has been used by the Administration for International Development (AID) to guide and supervise projects abroad which receive aid from the United States for the construction of low-income cooperative housing. Within the United States the FCH Company is used by the Federal Housing Administration to supervise federally-aided low-income housing cooperatives.

Most of the cooperative housing developments to date in the United States have been too costly for the very poor. But, in addition to the new, federally-assisted low-income housing cooperatives

---

23 United Housing Foundation, 465 Grand Street, New York, New York 10002.

24 12 U.S.C. 1715(e) (1964).

25 Foundation for Cooperative Housing, 1001 Fifteenth Street, N.W., Washington, D.C. 20005. FCH Company, same address.

there are three new applications of the cooperative method which promise to help solve some of the housing problems of the poor. In rural areas, the Farmer's Home Administration has had for years the authority to loan money on favorable terms to individuals with low incomes to buy modest homes or repair their present dwellings. The FHA recently began lending money for construction of groups of homes on a cooperative basis. These are variations of the plan to meet the needs of the group, but in general the prospective owners form a cooperative, purchase the necessary land, and furnish all the common or semi-skilled labor involved in constructing the homes. The Farmers Home Administration approves the plans in advance, furnishes a building supervisor and loans the money to pay for materials and skilled labor. Each man puts in a specified number of hours working with his fellow cooperators on each of their homes pursuant to a labor contract. He moves into a house with perhaps half the cost paid by his own labor, and with a low-interest, low monthly payment loan for the balance.[26]

In the cities where low-income people own their own homes, the cost of home repair and maintenance may be prohibitive. In the Pilsen area of Chicago, home owners have formed a cooperative which operates as a bargaining agency to obtain low-cost home repairs. This enables a community of home owners to maintain their community and prevent it from deteriorating into a slum.[27]

Another interesting cooperative housing development was the recent sale by the Chicago Housing Authority of a public housing project to a cooperative of tenants. The project, Racine Courts, built in 1950, was having some difficulty since many of its tenants had prospered over the years. Their incomes had risen above the maximum allowed for residence in the development but they could not afford the higher rents outside the project. The uniqueness of the new cooperative lies in the provision for a sliding scale of interest payments, so that families of lower income and larger families will pay a lower rate of interest than those with higher incomes or smaller families.[28]

It seems highly probable that cooperative housing for low-income residents of the inner city ghettos will be a major factor in the rebuilding which is so badly needed. This is a complicated

---

26 For more information contact Farmers Home Administration, U.S. Department of Agriculture, Washington, D.C. 20051.

27 For more information on the Pilsen project, contact The Cooperative League of the USA, 59 E. Van Buren St., Chicago, Illinois 60605.

28 *FCH News Briefs*, February, 1968.

problem and any interested group will have to seek the aid of the insurance, cooperative, labor or religious organizations which have sponsored cooperative housing projects. Such sponsors have the personnel with the technical skills to guide a prospective cooperative group through the maze of regulations, red tape and financial transactions involved in large real estate and construction projects. Guidance in securing the service and support of such an organization or sponsor is available through the National Association of Housing Cooperatives.[29]

### VIII. The Lawyer's Function in Cooperative Organization Among the Poor

Even a cursory examination of the variety and complexity of cooperative organizations makes it clear that most cooperative enterprises require experienced technical assistance. Initially they need inspiring but wise educational guidance to stimulate the study and understanding by the group of its needs before intelligent action to meet those needs may be undertaken. If the action indicated is a cooperative endeavor, advisees will need to understand what cooperation will require of them. These are the responsibilities of the educator-organizer and his sponsoring organization.

The lawyer also has an important role in this process. The problem of organizing a consumer cooperative of the poor is not solved by simply educating the poor until they are prepared for cooperative action and then incorporating. The most successful organizing procedure comes in short steps. First a little education, then a little action; another step in education, and the corresponding action. Action and education will reinforce each other until the group has acquired sufficient experience and capital to begin a larger business enterprise. Then it is time to incorporate. The lawyer has two functions during the educational process: first, to see that the group does not incorporate until its members thoroughly understand what they are doing; second, to see that they do not put off incorporation too long, and so unnecessarily jeopardize the capital and enthusiasm they are accumulating.

During this organization period, the attorney for the organizing group can perform a most valuable service. He can give some sound business advice under the guise of legal counsel:

1. He can point out the legal responsibility of the officers of

---

[29] National Association of Housing Cooperatives, 1012 14th Street, N.W., Washington, D.C. 20005.

the buying club to require payment in advance or upon delivery. This is necessary for their own protection and to prevent that most frequent cause of cooperative failure, uncontrolled credit.

2. He can stress the legal (and business) necessity of recording every member transaction from the start. The allocation of patronage savings is impossible without such records. Unexpected liability for income tax may be incurred without records of all transactions between the cooperative and the individual member.[30] It is not only the members of the cooperative who need this advice. The community action financers of initial organizational expenses of a cooperative venture should make it clear that any cooperative receiving the taxpayers' assistance must keep good records. Nothing creates more suspicion, doubt and hostility than failure to keep records that show where every penny of every member and every dollar of the government's investment has gone. In practice this means preparation of a monthly operating statement and balance sheet.

3. The attorney should be certain the by-laws require bonding of all employees responsible for handling funds, and insist upon prompt compliance with the requirement.

4. Finally, the attorney who is the established friend and protector of the cooperative can give this sound advice: "Get a good manager and pay him what he's worth." It may be necessary to advise the OEO officials as well as the poor. If this means going outside of the immediate community or hiring somebody who isn't within the "poverty guidelines," insist on it as good business and sound legal advice. Some OEO officials may not be happy about such counsel,

---

30 Generally distributions of a cooperative's net earnings to its patrons are not deductible unless they qualify for such treatment by meeting specific requirements. To be a qualified patronage dividend the amount paid to a patron by the cooperative association must be paid on the basis of the quantity or value of business done with or for the patron and be determined by reference to the net earnings of the association from business done with or for its patrons receiving similar distributions. INT. REV. CODE of 1954 § 1388(A). The patron may exclude patronage dividends from his gross income to the extent they are issued and based on his purchase of personal, living or family items. INT. REV. CODE of 1954 § 1385(B)(2). However, if he cannot identify the transaction or item on which a patronage dividend is distributed to him, he must generally treat it as ordinary income. Treas. Reg. § 1.1385-1(c)(iv)(1963). The importance of records of the transactions made is therefore readily apparent.

but the fact remains that the co-op manager and the co-op or OEO officials who share in hiring him are fiduciaries who handle money. A co-op must have a manager with experience whose reliability is beyond question.

The foregoing advice may go beyond the strict requirements of the law. But it is quite in keeping with the purposes of legal aid to the poor. For in a very real sense, the cooperative's attorney, like the cooperative's organizer, is a trustee—a trustee of the spirit of a people attempting to lift themselves out of poverty. That spirit can only be sustained by maintaining the highest business integrity and efficiency.